BREAKING FREE AND HEALING THE HEART WORKBOOK

Overcoming Obstacles to Healthy Relationships

SYDNEY GIENTY, M.A., LMHC

(Individual, Family, and Marriage Counselor)

Olympia, Washington 98502

(360) 943-9706

This is a work of fiction. All of the characters, names, incidents, organizations, and dialogue in this novel are either the products of the author's imagination or are used fictitiously.

WestBow Press books may be ordered through booksellers or by contacting:

WestBow Press
A Division of Thomas Nelson & Zondervan
1663 Liberty Drive
Bloomington, IN 47403
www.westbowpress.com
1 (866) 928-1240

ISBN: 978-1-5127-8046-8 (sc)
ISBN: 978-1-5127-8045-1 (e)

Library of Congress Control Number: 2017904918

Print information available on the last page.

WestBow Press rev. date: 04/10/2017

This book is dedicated to the Lord Jesus Christ,
who is the author and finisher of our faith.

Contents

Acknowledgments

The author wishes to acknowledge that without the help of my husband, children and many faithful friends this manuscript would not have been completed.

I have grown spiritually every step of the way and have learned more about Jesus and His love, power, and grace. I wish to thank my faithful, loving husband for supporting, encouraging, and instructing me as I undertook a task that seemed insurmountable. Through my children, God has taught me that His principles work, and He is faithful to fulfill His promises.

Throughout the writing of this manual, my friends have supported and helped me. They have edited, contributed insight, and encouraged me to keep going when it would have been easier to quit. I deeply appreciate those individuals who have been willing to share their testimonies about God's miraculous power in their lives.

May God bless each of you.

Foreword

I've been using Sydney's materials with my clients for years—ever since it helped me receive healing for my own emotional wounds. For years prior, I struggled with issues related to my own history of woundedness. Despite my best efforts, I could not seem to overcome the perpetual hurt that I carried inside. It was a pain that affected my ministry, my marriage, and my walk with God. I had already spent thousands of dollars in counseling fees and dozens of weeks of intense personal reflection. All of those counselors taught me something useful and even important about how to manage my pain. Sydney showed me how God would take it away for good. My journey in life was probably something like yours … really painful. I didn't see the use for Biblical counseling beyond what I had already received. After one more go around with my wife during a season of unemployment and financial struggles, I couldn't see what Sydney could do for me that all those previous counselors couldn't. I told my wife, "I don't want to spend more time and money on more ineffective counseling that's only going to dredge up a lot of pain as I spend weeks staring at my naval." But with my wife's pressure and the Holy Spirit's guidance, I relented. I am so glad I did! Going through this material and applying the principles that are taught has definitely been one of the best decisions of my life.

Beyond the freedom of releasing my personal baggage, I have experienced the joy of using this material and seeing life after life transformed as I witness the wounds of my own clients being completely erased. I've seen God work intensely in their lives as we apply the Scriptures to their situations. Old, crusty solders grow loving. Scared and guarded women grow bold. Broken lives and marriages get restored. It's exciting stuff, real early Church, New Testament Holy Spirit power. I know I am writing checks here that only God can cash, but how can I help it when I've seen Him work through the very same material in this book time and time again? You need to do the work like I did and apply this material to your life. I haven't been disappointed. I don't believe you will be either.

Chaplain Jason Haddock
United States Army

It was because of consistent years of marital difficulty and strife that my husband and I went to Sydney. Instead of working with us as a couple, she worked with us individually using Scripture to address our woundedness, and how that was affecting our outlook and behavior. The Holy Spirit used Sydney to show me I was developing a stony heart toward my husband. Many of the issues I thought were all him were really my own issues that I had been oblivious about, even after going to several other Christian counselors. When Sydney guided me through forgiving those who had caused my woundedness and prayed Jesus' healing over me, I felt God's love and presence wash over me like I had never known before. True inward, life-changing healing was the result. Issues I had struggled with for years were dissolved.

It has now been several years since that healing experience. Time has proven that this was not just a temporary thing. I don't have the anxiety, need to control, or destructive language that I used to have toward my husband and children. Where my marriage was once marked by strife, distance, high blood pressure, and accusations, it is now filled with love, unity, peace and grace. God used Sydney and her understanding and application of Scripture in a mighty way to heal my life and marriage. God wants to do this for you too. I praise God for this book and for how He is going to use it to heal many more lives.

Linda Haddock

Introduction

For many years, I have had the wonderful privilege of praying for many of God's people for emotional healing. I have seen God heal and restore individuals and couples in amazing ways. I have come to know my God as a loving Heavenly Father who meets His children's needs in a way that is always unique and special to them. The testimonies enclosed in this workbook reveal God's power and His uniqueness. Many times as I am praying for someone, I know that God is ministering to them, but I have no idea how. Sometimes God just brings a deep peace. Other times He gives them a vision, or they simply feel a deep release or a burden taken by the Spirit of God. Whatever God does, it is life changing and permanent. I can only praise Him for His faithfulness and abiding love. The greatest privilege in life is to serve our Lord and Master, Jesus Christ.

God wants to heal His children emotionally and physically, but the greatest healing comes when we receive God's Son, Jesus, as our personal Lord and Savior.

To receive Jesus into your life and have the assurance that your sins are forgiven and you will spend eternity in heaven with Him, simply requires that you ask Him to come into your life and be Lord of your life. Say the following prayer:

> *"Jesus, I acknowledge that I am a sinner. I ask You to forgive me of all my sins and to come into my life. I believe that You died for me on the cross, and that You rose again on the third day that I might be saved and my sins washed away. I know that You will come again, and I will live with You forever. I choose this day to live for You, Jesus. Thank You for saving me from my sins."*

> "For God did not send his Son into the world to condemn the world, but to save the world through him. Whoever believes in him is not condemned, but whoever does not believe stands condemned already because they have not believed in the name of God's one and only Son. This is the verdict: Light has come into the world, but people loved darkness instead of light because their deeds were evil. Everyone who does evil hates the light, and will not come into the light for fear that

> their deeds will be exposed. But whoever lives by the truth comes into the light, so that it may be seen plainly that what they have done has been done in the sight of God." (John 3:17-21 NIV)

> "For God so loved the world that he gave his one and only Son, that whoever believes in him shall not perish but have eternal life." (John 3:16 NIV)

> "If you declare with your mouth, 'Jesus is Lord,' and believe in your heart that God raised him from the dead, you will be saved. For it is with your heart that you believe and are justified, and it is with your mouth that you profess your faith and are saved. As Scripture says, 'Anyone who believes in him will never be put to shame.'" (Rom. 10:9-11 NIV)

As the scripture says, "Anyone who believes in Him will never be put to shame." Trust in Jesus today, and ask Him to come into your heart. The testimonies you will read about in this workbook are the miracles that God has done for those who have surrendered their heart to Jesus and have been saved from their sins by a living, ever present, loving Lord and Savior. Will you join them and receive a relationship with the Lord that will change your life? Ask Him today to come into your heart and be Lord of your life.

Beauty for Ashes—Testimony

A young woman who was broken emotionally, spiritually and physically writes the following story. God met her right where she was and completely set her free. She tells only part of her story here, but what she shares gives you a glimpse of how God met her in a powerful way. God did for her what no human could ever do. He not only healed her, but He miraculously revealed His power and presence to her. God will do the same for you because He loves you and died for you.

"The Spirit of the Sovereign Lord is on me,
because the Lord has anointed me to proclaim good news to the poor.
He has sent me to bind up the brokenhearted."
—Isaiah 61:1 NIV

In my state of mourning, I had given up on God. I had decided that He had given up on me a long time ago, and now I was done with Him. If God was trustworthy, all-knowing, and all-powerful, then why didn't He care about me and the pain I was in? Anything to do with God angered me. At church, the praise made my heart feel like stone. Was all hope gone? I had been in church my whole life. I had even been in the ministry. But I never dared to confront God with the truly hard questions. *Where was God? Who was God?* And why didn't I have a childhood filled with love, laughter, and innocence? Little did I know that Christ would soon be blessing me with comfort to my soul.

"To proclaim freedom for the captives
and release from darkness for the prisoners."
—Isaiah 61:1 NIV

I lived through a unique captivity where the sins of past generations were carried onto me. I was born into a family that was already maxed out emotionally and financially. I grew up in a house filled with anger, rage, deceit, and chaos. It was survival of the fittest. Being the youngest, I wasn't the fittest. But by the grace of God, I was a survivor. Growing up I never felt I belonged or was wanted in the family. My parents were struggling with their own lives, unable to give me the attention I longed for. I learned in most part to stay out of the way. I watched from an emotional distance, wanting someone to notice there was a hurting child who needed a tight hug, who needed a gentle smile, and who needed to know that life wasn't going to destroy her. In the midst of all the anger and chaos, I would try to disappear, only to be found by my older brother who physically, emotionally, and sexually abused me. My brother would tell me that I was what was wrong with our family. "It wasn't like this before you were born," he would say. It was like a sword through my heart. "You don't deserve to live for what you've done to our family, and someday I will kill you." And I believed him. He would beat me if I crossed him, or at times he would hit me for entering the room he was in. He would dig a hole in the backyard to my measurements and put me in the hole. It was so narrow that I couldn't move my arms from my sides or bend my knees. I would think to myself, "Is he going to kill me this time?" I quickly learned to disassociate and not feel. *Do you see me God? Do you know I am here? Do you care?* Over the years I learned to survive. But with the survival came a lot of baggage. The abuse became my secret, even from God. No one was to be trusted. My secret bored to the core of my being. Every action and reaction I had was to protect the little girl inside of me who was frozen in a moment of time and couldn't escape her own terror. I became angry at God instead of being angry at those who hurt me. Why didn't anyone love me? I believed that God didn't even love me.

Through a series of events, I ended up counseling with Sydney. I was angry with God and felt there was no hope left for me. I would allow others to pray for me, believing that it wouldn't hurt me and that maybe I would even feel better. I asked Sydney, "Where was God in the middle of my pain?" She said I would have to ask God for myself. I had a lot of wounds. Sydney assured me that God knew about each one and that He was more than capable of healing each one. She instructed me to journal about specific hurtful incidents that had happened to me, and then we would pray and ask God to take away the pain. We prayed, and God met me in ways I would have never imagined. Jesus reached down and placed a gift in my mind—my place of torment. It was as if I was watching a movie where I could not only see but feel both emotionally and physically.

"To comfort all who mourn, and provide for those
who grieve in Zion—to bestow on them a crown of beauty
instead of ashes, the oil of joy instead of mourning,
and a garment of praise instead of a spirit of despair."
—Isaiah 61:2–3 NIV

I saw a hospital room. A woman was lying on a bed, giving birth. The room was filled with motion and activity. There were lights, instruments, and a sterile coldness. Jesus appeared in all of His beautiful perfection, anxiously anticipating the birth. A baby was born. That baby was me. As the connecting cords were severed, Jesus reached down gently and picked up the baby. The hospital room and all of its activity simply faded away. The baby was being cradled in Jesus' arms. His gaze held on her face. His eyes told the story as He took in the fullness of her. The love that welled from the core of His being went into the baby. The pride then quickened, and He said, "She is mine." He knew the gifts and aspirations that would be uniquely hers. He yearned for the relationship that would be distinctively theirs. His eyes bestowed on her the depth of His longing and love for her. His soft tears of joy resoundingly declared, "Rejoice, my daughter has been born." Jesus stood there, veiled in white, holding my newborn form with gentle tenderness. His eyes locked on mine, reaching to my soul. I knew I was wanted and loved.

God had really met me right where I was, and He loved me. This special experience gave me hope to move on. I had to deal with the wounds from the sexual abuse. This was a little more intense. This was my secret. This is where everyone had failed me. This was the one that I wasn't so sure there would be anything left of me when it was exposed. Sydney and I prayed and cried. And I forgave my brother. I did not forgive him because he asked for forgiveness, but because I was bound by the unforgiveness. It was eating me alive. But I still had the question, "Where was God in the middle of my pain?"

I Was There All the Time

Jesus came to me once again. The room held a dark evil. A silent terror. I was frozen, unable to move. The agony that was mine ate to the core of my being. I had known evil for so long, and it still brought panic and horror to me. There were others in the room. They were going about their daily lives without a care, and they didn't seem to notice me or the terror that rendered me helpless. Why wouldn't they help me? Why did they not feel the terror that occupied the room? Maybe they did. Could it be that in recognizing the darkness of such evil, it would have consumed them? *Jesus, where are You? If anyone could free me from this horror, You could. Are You "all-knowing"? Do You know I am here, God? Or, do You, too, turn Your face away from the sight of my agony? Where are You, God? Am I not worthy of Your time? Not worth saving? Why won't anyone love me?* As I lay in the bed where I was being violated, frozen with terror, Jesus appeared in the room. All power and authority radiated from His being. He reached down to where I lay, and my captor's limbs were rendered useless. Jesus picked me up and held me to His chest. With His strong arms around me and my face cradled in His neck, I could feel His heart break. The intense love He had for me, and His grieving pain for what I had endured, was beyond words. Yet in that moment, His love and care were conveyed to my soul. Jesus replied, "I was there all the time." I put my arms around His neck, and peace filled my heart. He was indeed my Savior.

God healed the torment of that room. My memory of the abuse isn't gone, but the pain of it is. The next day as I heard praise music, it no longer made me hard; it brought peace to my soul like a healing ointment. Then Sydney and I came to another counseling time. I was dealing with not understanding God as my daddy. I felt defective. Couldn't I even have that part of God? God gave me another gift. He went directly to the wounded place, and this is what He showed me.

The King

I was looking for a daddy to hold me, protect me, and call me his own. My search seemed in vain. I continued nonetheless. I stopped my search when I saw a throne. It was massive. Gold with precious stones adorned it. The sight of it suggested omnipotence. It was the throne of God. God sat on the throne in all of His majesty. His appearance was that of power. A warrior, victorious over any foe. His unquestionable strength showed in His powerful form. Wisdom radiated from His being. Yet His eyes were those of compassion and tenderness. He was clothed in royalty. His gold crown proclaimed His Lordship. This was the King of kings. He looked at me with a smile on His face. He reached to where I was and lifted me unto Himself. He sat me on His knee and held me in His strong arms. He said, "You are my princess."

A joy filled my heart as I realized He had chosen me. I felt safe and at peace. He was proud to claim me as His own. I knew at that moment I was wrapped around His heart. I, too, was clothed in royalty. Adorned with a purple robe and a diamond tiara. I was a princess. More importantly, I was His princess. My search was over. This One for whom all praise is due. The Lord of all. The Mighty Warrior. The King of kings is my Daddy.

I was not only being healed, but I was starting a new relationship with God. Not one I controlled, but one He controlled. Sydney and I prayed that any stronghold Satan would have on my thoughts, wounds or emotions would be gone. Since all my wounds were in my mind and my heart, that is where Satan would attack me. And that is exactly where God chose to meet me and kick Satan in the teeth. During our prayer, another memory of abuse came to mind. Then, Jesus gave me another vision.

Peace and Wholeness

I was a small girl. I was in a hole dug to my measurements. The hole was narrow. My arms were bound to my sides by the tight walls of dirt surrounding me. My legs were unable to bend. I was barely able to breathe the fresh air. I wanted out but was unable to move or help myself. *Would I die here? Would he let me out?* The mental anguish was unbearable. It was at that moment Jesus appeared. I knew He would help me. I was so weary I wasn't even able to call out to Him. But, He knew I was there. He bent down and put His hands into the hole where I had been standing for so long. I could feel His strong hands under my arms as He lifted me out of that hole. Relief washed over me as He held my small form in His arms. When He helped me stand up, I was no longer a child but an adult. Jesus took a step back and looked full into my face. Then I noticed He held something in His hands. The object radiated—red with white brilliance. *Does He want me to take it? Is it a ruby? What is it?* He reached out to give it to me. I stepped back and shook my head. He drew the brilliant object to His chest and said, "I will take care of it for you." Then, Jesus lifted me into His arms. I was a child again. He walked to a cross and laid me at the foot of it. It was beautiful and quiet there. A sweet aroma of flowers filled the air. I curled up at the base of the cross like a small kitten. I found peace and slept.

Sometime later Sydney and I prayed again. Once more Jesus came to me holding the brilliant object, which shone brightly on His face. He held it out to me. Again I stepped back. But this time I was intrigued. I wanted to see what it was. I leaned forward to look into His hands, where He held the most beautiful heart. It was red like a ruby, but brilliantly white at the same time. It was so clean and pure. It had no breaks, no chips, and no cloudiness to obscure its wholeness and value. Again Jesus offered it to me. This beautiful and precious gift was for me. I could hardly believe it! Happiness welled up in me as I reached for the heart. Our hands met, and we stood there together for a fraction of time holding this most beautiful precious gift, my new heart. The brilliance from it radiated through my being. Jesus stepped back and once again looked full into my face. Our eyes met and my soul cried out, "Thank you!" The peace and wholeness I so longed for was mine.

> "They will be called oaks of righteousness,
> a planting of the Lord for the display of his splendor."
> —Isaiah 61:3 NIV

I share this with you to rejoice in the splendor of a trustworthy, all-knowing, all-powerful God. A God who lovingly freed the child in my mind, and filled the hole in my soul.

Commit Yourself to Healing

Throughout time, mankind has walked down many avenues to try to obtain happiness and fulfillment. For a season, many of the paths taken or the decisions made seem pleasurable. Fleshly desires are gratified and all seems well. The problem is that meeting our fleshly desires brings us into sinful behavior and sinful responses. If we have accepted Jesus as our Lord and Savior and have chosen to walk with Him, the flesh must be put to death and the life of Jesus resurrected within us. This death and resurrection are a process and require that we honestly look at ourselves and choose to bring our lives into obedience to God's Word.

> "In the same way, count yourselves dead to sin but alive to God in Christ Jesus. Therefore do not let sin reign in your mortal body so that you obey its evil desires. Do not offer any part of yourself to sin as an instrument of wickedness, but rather offer yourselves to God as those who have been brought from death to life; and offer every part of yourself to him as an instrument of righteousness. For sin shall no longer be your master, because you are not under the law, but under grace." (Rom. 6:11-14 NIV)

> "There is a way that appears to be right, but in the end it leads to death." (Prov. 14:12 NIV)

Sin rules and reigns here on earth. None of us is immune to its influence. Those who walk in disobedience, as well as those who walk in obedience to God, have been wounded by the sin of others and by their own sin. Sometimes the wounds of sin are so devastating that an individual hides them deep within their heart and chooses not to feel or acknowledge their pain. Oftentimes there is the belief: "If I ignore my pain it will go away," or "I just need to claim God's Word, then I am healed." This approach to woundedness does not work, nor is it biblical.

> "Therefore, confess your sins to each other and pray for each other so that you may be healed. The prayer of a righteous man is powerful and effective." (James 5:16 NIV)

For emotional healing to take place, the following events must take place in our lives. We must:

1. Be willing to look at our sin.
2. Look at our sinful attitudes and behaviors when others have sinned against us.
3. Confess our sin to God and sometimes to another.
4. Receive prayer for healing.

When woundedness has been deep and possibly ongoing for years, it is difficult to dredge up and look at the old wounds. Our natural tendency as humans is to proceed with our lives, forgetting the past. The problem is the past is never really forgotten unless it is healed by Jesus. Secretly hiding the past within us is not healing. God's Word says He will reveal those things hidden in darkness and set us free. Our freedom comes from looking at what is hidden in the dark recesses of our heart.

We must acknowledge that God, and only God, can forgive and heal us of those deep feelings that we've held against those who hurt us. True freedom, wholeness, and healing are evidenced when the pain is gone and forgiveness is in operation. Then, we are free and able to share our hurt with others and bless those who have hurt us. To reach this level of healing requires allowing the Holy Spirit to show us what is truly in our heart. The Word says, "The heart is deceitful above all things … Who can understand it?" (Jer. 17:9 NIV). Because of this wickedness, we must be willing to invite the Lord to reveal to us what is in our heart, what we really believe, and what sin rules and reigns in our lives. Permitting the Lord to do this requires a willingness to be stripped down in order to be built up in Him. This is a painful process, but a very rewarding one!

When we have been badly wounded, there isn't much enthusiasm in allowing God to further open us up and reveal what is hidden within our souls. This process connects us once again with PAIN. Many say, "I don't want to feel the pain again." The truth is, they are walking in pain everyday of their life if their heart has not been healed. If they are numb to their emotions, they may not feel the pain, but their belief system and their actions toward others will be evidenced in ways that defile them and wound others.

Unhealed hearts become stony or hardened hearts. A stony heart is the result of woundedness. Woundedness causes us to erect ineffective walls of protection around our hearts so we cannot be hurt again. These same walls prevent us from freely giving or receiving love. They also keep us from trusting. Mistrust increases the walls of protection and hardness of heart. Many times we do not truly believe that God will protect, help, or heal us. Our heart is "closed" down as the wounds fester in our heart and make us miserable. God, however, promised He will heal us!

> "The righteous cry out, and the Lord hears them; he delivers them from all their troubles. The Lord is close to the brokenhearted and saves those who are crushed in spirit. A righteous man may have many troubles, but the Lord delivers him from them all." (Ps. 34:17-19 NIV)

The first step to healing is taking God at His Word. He says He will heal us. He always keeps His promises! We need to place our confidence in God's Word. By faith, we are to trust Him to come through for us.

> "I face your Temple as I worship, giving thanks to you for all your loving-kindness and your faithfulness, for your promises are backed by all the honor of your name." (Ps. 138:2 TLB)

> "Hear my prayer, O Lord; answer my plea because you are faithful to your promises." (Ps. 142:1 TLB)

> "Lord, if you keep in mind our sins then who can ever get an answer to his prayers? But you forgive! What an awesome thing this is! That is why I wait expectantly, trusting God to help, for he has promised." (Ps. 130:3-4 TLB)

> "You are my refuge and my shield, and your promises are my only source of hope … I have thoroughly tested your promises and that is why I love them so much … I stay awake through the night to think about your promises." (Ps. 119:114, 140, 148 TLB)

We cannot change our heart or "will" it to be healed. It is God who must do the healing. We just have to be willing vessels, permitting Him to do it. God is faithful, and He will do the work if we ask. Emotional healing is a process! It is not simply praying to forgive those who have hurt us. That is certainly necessary, but it is not the first step. The first step is finding out what is truly in our heart toward those who have hurt or defiled us. By looking at our past and what has happened to us, we can enter the first step of the healing process. We must identify those who have defiled us and how we feel about them. Then, we must look at the sinful attitudes and behaviors in our own lives that result from these past events. Next, we choose to ask God's forgiveness for our sin and forgive those who have sinned against us.

This process may appear simple, but it isn't. It takes time, commitment and energy to look at our woundedness, attitudes, belief system and behaviors. God's purpose is to build His Christ-like character within each of us. As we look at our sinful behaviors and responses, choose to bring them to the cross and the cleansing blood of Jesus. When we make this decision, we are dying to our flesh and becoming like Jesus. As our sinful nature dies, we can then live and walk in the Spirit.

> "So I say, walk by the Spirit, and you will not gratify the desires of the flesh. For the flesh desires what is contrary to the Spirit, and the Spirit what is contrary to the flesh. They are in conflict with each other, so that you are not to do whatever you want. But if you are led by the Spirit, you are not under the law.
>
> The acts of the flesh are obvious: sexual immorality, impurity and debauchery; idolatry and witchcraft; hatred, discord, jealousy, fits of rage, selfish ambition, dissensions, factions and envy; drunkenness, orgies, and the like. I warn you, as I did before, that those who live like this will not inherit the kingdom of God.
>
> But the fruit of the Spirit is love, joy, peace, forbearance, kindness, goodness, faithfulness, gentleness and self-control. Against such things there is no law. Those who belong to Christ Jesus have crucified the flesh with its passions and desires. Since we live by the Spirit, let us keep in step with the Spirit." (Gal. 5:16-25 NIV)

Satan is able to get his hook into us through our woundedness. He uses unresolved hurt, pain, and unforgiveness to lead, control, and direct us. Unresolved woundedness also produces bad fruit in our life. These sinful attitudes, behaviors, and wounds lead us down destructive paths. As these areas are presented to Jesus, through the power of the cross and the blood of Jesus we are released and set free emotionally. We are also freed from Satan's clutches!

Journaling is a very important part of working through healing. It helps us get in touch with what is in our heart as the Holy Spirit brings up attitudes and issues. Many individuals receive some healing as they journal. Just thinking about our wounds does not get us in touch with our heart. Journaling gives us more understanding about how we feel and what has happened to us emotionally. Journaling also helps reveal issues hidden deep within our heart. Individuals often tell me, "I didn't know that was in my heart." As you proceed through this workbook, journal as requested. God will reveal and do amazing healings.

This workbook has been written to be used as a guide to help you come into healing. Everyone who has seriously asked God to heal them and worked through the steps toward healing has been healed. God is faithful to perform His Word. Remember what He says in His Word, He will heal and always keeps His promises. Welcome to the path of healing—God has great things in store for you!

Offenses

The healing process must first begin by understanding that *offenses* wound our heart. Both the Old and New Testaments outline the definition of an offense.

- New Testament Greek meaning of *offenses* from Strong's Concordance: Snare, scandal, cause of displeasure or sin, occasion to fall, thing that offends, stumbling block, to strike at, surge against, trip up, beat upon, stumble at.
- Old Testament Hebrew meaning of *offenses* from Strong's Concordance: A stumbling block, obstacle, enticement, cause to fall, ruin, a crime, punishment of sin, bind, to pervert, destroy, to writhe in pain, bring forth corruption, destroy.

When offenses are not dealt with, the following problems may occur:

- We are led astray (Gen. 20:2-11).
- We lose out on what God has for us (1 Kings 18:14).
- We add sin upon sin in our life (2 Chron. 28:13).
- We bear the blame for others' sin (Jer. 37:18).
- We become desolate or are punished. This leads to idol worship (Hosea 13:1).
- We are tripped up and miss the power of God's Word (Matt. 13:21).
- We can't receive from the Lord (Matt. 13:57).
- We stumble, are entrapped or bring displeasure to others.
- We fall into sin and hate one another. We go astray and lead others astray (Matt. 24:10).
- We desert the Lord when pride is involved (Mark 14:29; Dan. 4).
- We can be wrongly accused resulting in hurt (Acts 25:11).
- We stumble and cause bloodshed/murder. It damages our conscience (1 Sam. 25:31).

Physical Effects:

- Migraine headaches
- Pre-menstrual syndrome (P.M.S.)
- Back problems—bones groan
- Weight problems
- Ulcers
- High blood pressure
- Nervous system problems
- Sleep disturbances
- Use of medication—legal/illegal
- Addictive behavior
- Sexual dysfunction

Repeated offenses cause us to believe lies such as:

- I am a failure. I am inadequate. I am defective.
- I must be perfect to receive approval.
- I am stupid, ugly, lazy, etc…
- Nobody wants me.
- I don't have the ability to succeed.
- If others really get to know me, they will not like or love me.
- God doesn't exist or doesn't love me.

Offenses cause children to suffer and struggle. Children who have not bonded appropriately to parents and did not receive nurturing in the early years or did not feel wanted, struggle in the following areas:

- Feel rejected, unloved, unwanted.
- Accept the message that they are a failure; not as good as they should be.
- Wish they had born a boy/girl.
- Learn to live a lie—may tell lies to cover up the truth to hide their pain.
- Carry tremendous guilt for not meeting others' expectations.
- Take on adult roles to win approval from parents.
- Take on the responsibility for the dysfunction in the family.
- Judge themselves without mercy and never feel good enough. "I cannot make a mistake."

- Never learned to play or have fun.
- Often have difficulty with intimate relationships.
- Constantly seek approval and affirmation, often ending up feeling more rejected.
- Develop a sense of shame and distrust toward others.
- Believe that "If God is like my parents, I don't want Him."
- Believe that "I will be abandoned."
- Believe that "I can never please God"

Trust

When offenses take place, the first response in the heart is to not trust. As we go through life and others offend and wound us, our distrust increases. To come into healing, we must be willing to open our heart and trust again. Basic trust does not mean the "ability to believe another," but the capacity to hold the heart open to others and to life, especially when we cannot believe others intend well.[1]

Basic trust is the fundamental building block in all human relationships. We learn basic trust from affectionate touch, or we fail to learn it. We get true or false messages about ourselves from previous experiences. If our heart has not learned to trust, we may close our heart to God and others.[2]

A closed heart or *stony heart* cannot receive or freely give love. A stony heart is the result of *inner vows, bitter-root judgments* and *bitter-root expectancies.*

> "And I will give you a new heart—I will give you new and right desires—and put a new spirit within you. I will take out your stony hearts of sin and give you new hearts of love. And I will put my Spirit within you so that you will obey my laws and do whatever I command." (Ezek. 36:26-27 TLB)

> "The heart is the most deceitful thing there is, and desperately wicked. No one can really know how bad it is. Only the Lord knows! He searches all hearts and examines deepest motives so he can give to each person his right reward, according to his deeds—how he has lived." (Jer. 17:9-10 TLB)

A stony heart prevents us from:

- Receiving love, affection and acceptance from others.
- Giving Christ-like love to others.

- Loving, which leaves us open to bitterness and hatred.
- Having oneness and spiritual unity in a marriage.
- Having a fulfilled relationship with God.
- Fully understanding or receiving from God's Word. Our personal spirit is in captivity.

To be healed of distrust, we need to look at the messages we received as a child. This does not mean that our parents intended to wound us, but that our spirit received messages that wounded us. The goal is not to judge or criticize our parents, but to look at what went into our heart and to examine our sinful responses. To understand what our wounds are, we must look at why we do not trust. The following are some of the reasons we have a problem trusting:

- There was verbal abuse in the home.
- We or someone in our home was physically or sexually abused.
- We were neglected. Our basic needs were not met.
- There were broken promises over and over again.
- Our opinions were not considered valid or important.
- There was little or no quality time together. Consequently, we were given the message that we were not significant or of value.
- here was name-calling or derogatory remarks made that shamed or wounded our spirit. The messages we received were that we are a failure, worthless, unimportant, unlovable, unwanted, or rejected
- Our parents lied to us. We believed that to protect ourselves we had to lie to feel safe. We got mixed messages whether we told the truth or lied. This resulted in being confused about how we should behave and what we should believe.

If you have wounded someone's spirit, the Lord may want to use you to bring that person into healing. If that is the case, the following steps will help the wounded individual begin to believe and trust you.

- Be a person of your word. Do what you say you will do.
- Build the wounded individual up by consistently giving them words of encouragement and affirmation.
- Do not lie.
- Be consistent in your behavior.
- Do not put your needs or feelings first. You must have a servant's heart.

- In those areas where you have wounded another, repent and ask for forgiveness.
- Be willing to restore what you have taken. Give in the way that will be meaningful to the other, not to you.
- Allow the other to heal, as you consistently love the person.

For those individuals who have not been restored by the one who wounded them, they need to be brought into healing by the love of others.

- Trust is restored through loving care and affection from others.
- Trust is restoral through healing prayer from others.
- Trust is restored by learning to trust God with your life.
- Trust is restored by claiming through faith God's promises in His Word.

A stony heart is healed by:

- *Repentance* of sinful attitudes, including inner vows, bitter-root judgments and bitter-root expectancies.
- *Forgiveness* toward those who have hurt, rejected or abused us.
- *Asking God* to take away our heart of stone and give us a heart of flesh (love).
- *Praying* for healing of our heart in all the areas we have been hurt.
- *Applying* and *receiving* God's promises of restoration and healing.

An individual with a stony heart should not pray for their healing alone. One of the main characteristics of a stony heart is closing others out emotionally and isolating oneself. For healing to take place, we must let others pray for us until the child heart learns it is truly loved. Then, the child heart can truly open up to others.

If we have learned basic trust, we can enter freely into the give and take of sharing emotions, thoughts and space with others. If not, we cannot.

When we do not trust God, we are saying:

- God, I cannot depend on you to take care of or protect me.
- God, you do not have my best interest at heart.
- I am better able to lead and direct my life than you are.
- God's Word is not true.
- God is a liar.
- I can protect myself better than God can.
- I will rescue me.
- Prayer does not have much power and is of no effect.

- God does not answer prayer.
- God will not come through for me.
- God does not keep His promises.
- My ways are better than God's ways.
- I know what is best for me.
- The walls I have put up are what really protect me.

Psalm 91 states that:

- God will cover and protect us.
- He will be our refuge.
- God will be our shield.
- We will not walk in fear or terror.
- Disaster will not overcome us.
- No harm will befall us.
- No disaster will come near our tent.
- Angels will guard us in all our ways; they will lift us up so that we do not strike our foot against a stone.
- God will rescue us.
- God will protect us, if we call on Him.
- God will answer us, deliver and honor us.
- We will have a long life and receive God's salvation.

BASIC TRUST

I JUST CAN'T DWELL IN THE PAST
MY PARENTS DID THE BEST THEY COULD
I'VE FORGIVEN THEM FOR ALL THEY'VE DONE
I'M UNLOVED...
I'M UNWANTED...
NOBODY CARES ABOUT ME...
I'M NOT IMPORTANT...

Trust Assignment

Define trust:

What must we have in life for trust to develop in our heart?

If our heart is not able to trust, what may happen in our relationships with God and others?

What is a stony heart, and what three things do we do if we have a stony heart?

1.

2.

3.

A stony heart prevents us from:

1.

2.

3.

4.

5.

6.

Explain Ezekiel 36:26 and how it applies to you.

Basic trust is restored by:

1.

2.

3.

A stony heart is healed by:

1.

2.

3.

4.

5.

How do you tell the difference between what you think and what you feel?

What childhood incidents have happened to you that resulted in you not trusting?

Why did you determine to close or harden your heart?

What has been the effect of closing or hardening your heart in your life?

How has closing your heart affected your relationship with your spouse, family, or close friends?

What scares you about opening up your heart to God and others?

What consequences have you experienced that have broken your heart because of not trusting others?

Becoming vulnerable can be very risky. What is God's promise to you if you open up to others and risk getting hurt?

Write down and memorize three scripture verses that will help you open your heart and be vulnerable to others.

To whom do you need to open your heart? What steps are you going to take to begin trusting and become vulnerable?

What are the risks?

According to God's Word, what is His promise to you if you are obedient to Him?

Trust Journal Assignment

Identify who hurt you. Journal about one individual at a time.

Next, start writing down hurtful incidents and how they made you feel. If your hurt and pain was in your childhood, write from the child's perspective. Write how you felt about the incident, not what you thought about it. You want to get in touch with your heart.

Then, journal about how this woundedness has affected your life.

Begin to identify your actual and false belief system about yourself, others and God. Write it down.

Hope Against All Odds—Testimony

The following testimony is the story of an individual who learned to trust.

Jeremiah 29:10 says, "'For I know the plans I have for you,' declares the Lord, 'plans to prosper you and not to harm you, plans to give you hope and a future'" (NIV). Up until a few years ago, my entire adult life had been a series of poor decisions. I made choices based on a skewed belief system—one that falsely represented my value and worth. Once I became grounded in who I am in Christ, I was able to make decisions for myself that were in alignment with both God's Word and will for my life. It changed me. It changed my whole life. I know that no tear is ever wasted, and God is able to re-purpose our pain for His glory.

As a child I had a strained relationship with my biological father. Growing up, I lacked security and boundaries. I became a woman who made choices based out of that lack, especially in regard to companionship. My past taught me that men were not trustworthy. I mistakenly believed this thought process to be wisdom, when in fact the reason I lacked trust was because I was broken. My insecurity led to a constant quest for validation. I had convinced myself that the world wasn't trustworthy. The truth was, I didn't consider myself to be trustworthy.

Time brought clarity. It became clear to me that before I could truly trust others, I must first learn how to trust, love and respect myself. A life of wholeness must be the first goal, but I didn't know how to achieve it. I hadn't yet realized that apart from God there could be no wholeness. There could be no true healing. I wish that I had learned this lesson early in life, but that is not my story.

I'd been living with one foot in and the other foot out of my Christian walk. I'd made compromises in an effort to be validated by others. I'd been juggling hats and faking the façade of being enough. It was exhausting! I would pray and surrender my behaviors to the Lord, only to fail in my efforts.

I was stuck in this cycle that confirmed what I had always feared. I wasn't loveable unless I was "doing good." Fast forward to 2010. I hadn't been in a relationship for several years—better to be alone than to make such a significant decision unwisely. Ultimately, that's what I believed. I could not be trusted to let wisdom lead me in choosing a mate. This long hiatus from dating gave me the false illusion of independence, strength, and newfound self-esteem. In reality, all I had done was suppress my emotional pain with avoidance. But the truth was, being in a relationship was more important to me than almost everything else. My worth was tied up in belonging to someone. My desire to belong and the disillusionment that accompanied it, led me to believe that it was time to get "back in the game."

I met my first husband on a Christian online dating site. He was my Prince Charming, or so I thought. You know the saying, "If it looks like a duck, swims like a duck, and quacks like a duck, then it probably is a duck." Well, I can tell you from experience that it's not ALWAYS true. My "prince" was all I had hoped for, until he wasn't. His charm was one of deception.

In 2 Timothy 3:6-7 we read, "They are the kind who worm their way into homes and gain control over gullible women, who are loaded down with sins and are swayed by all kinds of evil desires, always learning but never able to come to a knowledge of the truth" (NIV). The Bible also tells us in Proverbs 4:23 that we should guard our hearts. I didn't do that. My hunger for acceptance and belonging made me careless.

I found myself in deep waters, wading through depression and disbelief. How had this happened? How had I gotten it so wrong, again? This time it was a marriage—a covenant. It appeared my marriage was on track to fail. I was on my way to becoming the one thing that I never wanted to be: divorced. I was at rock bottom and the obvious questions were unavoidable. What about my future? What about my children?

In my 15 years of experience as a registered nurse, I have seen manipulation, and I have dealt with different personalities and conflict on a regular basis. But it was different. Those scenarios were "theirs" and I was on the outskirts. Now, I was no longer on the periphery of a manipulative situation. I was smack dab in the middle of it. Fortunately, what those experiences as an observer taught me is that I could not fix this alone. Despite our desires for independence, we are not meant to. I knew that things had to change, so I put forth the effort to find both a great church and a fantastic counselor.

I would like to say that I had a huge surge of confidence and stood up for myself overnight. What I can tell you is that I stuck with the process even when it was difficult, and my children had a lot to do with that! Things started looking up for me when I began to seek out healthy female relationships at church. I finally had a mentor and girlfriends who were committed to "doing life" with me. It made such a huge difference! Finally, despite my tumultuous circumstances, my life was filled with unexplainable peace and joy!

I was challenged to read the Bible, marinate in God's Word daily and embrace what God said about me. I would like to say it was easy, but it wasn't because I was used to "doing things" to be accepted. Merely accepting God's love instead of trying to earn it was a foreign concept.

There were obstacles and there always will be. As I stayed in the Word, my faith grew. As my faith grew, my self-worth grew. As my self-worth grew, I realized that I was no longer susceptible to manipulation. That didn't mean the struggle was over. Far from it. But I was doing things differently. I was relying on God to make me an overcomer instead of relying on myself. Different tactic = different outcome. I had to be willing to commit to a drastic change. I had to trust my counselor and mentor. What they spoke lined up with the Word of God, so I knew that I could trust them entirely.

Through it all I had embraced the rest and peace that came from relying on my heavenly Father. Ultimately, the key was learning how to discover my identity in Christ. When I found out who God said I was and who He created me to be, I learned to believe those things. I was no longer willing to settle. God wanted the best for me, and I was finally able to come alongside Him and want it for myself as well.

Healing is a process. During my healing I tried things that I had never tried before. I started to write in a journal, which was very cathartic for me. Taking care of myself first was also a new concept for me. I began to truly see the importance of self-care, so I chose to eat healthier and exercise. This, matched with my new understanding of my worth, helped me to lose all of the weight that I had gained during my marriage. I also began serving in my church. I learned that helping others while you yourself are in need is constructive and healthy. I continued in counseling and grew in relationships. I knew it was wise to keep my circle of close friends small during my struggle. The process of traversing through life's struggles aren't meant to be shared with everyone. I always encourage people to be in prayer about who God wants to bring alongside them during those seasons. It will be people who will pray for you because praying friends are so important.

I felt stronger as time passed. My confidence and courage grew, even today it continues to grow. My mentor recently said she barely recognizes me and for all the right reasons. Doubt, shame, depression, heartache, low self-esteem, anxiety and worry, they have all been shed. They have been replaced with joy, peace, health and wholeness. God is the great restorer.

What the enemy meant for my destruction has been the very thing that has enabled me to help women who are struggling with the same things with which I have struggled. I want to encourage woman to get help if they are feeling isolated or abused. Honestly, going through these things was a painful lesson, but it was also my biggest catalyst for change. Pain, as it turns out, is a good motivator.

One of greatest decisions I made was to invest in counseling. I could no longer "do enough" to fix this mess. I went to see Sydney. She had immediate insight into my situation. She was able to identify the abuse cycles (verbal and emotional). For the first time, I felt validated. I wasn't crazy. I was, however, broken. I had to do the work. As I continued in counseling, Sydney helped me go back to the root of my painful brokenness. Through prayer and counseling, I was able to identify and unearth the deep roots of pain. You have to address the root to heal, and you can't do it alone. I was on my way to breaking free!

Forgiveness

When we have been offended and have pain in our heart, we must forgive those who have hurt us and forgive ourselves for our failures. Unforgiveness destroys and brings bondage. God says we are to forgive others as He has forgiven us. Who can really understand the forgiveness that God extends to us? The depth of God's love and forgiveness are beyond man's comprehension. Without God's love and forgiveness we would be eternally lost and continue to live with the consequences of our sin and the sins others commit against us. God, who is holy, cannot tolerate sin. He says, "I will cleanse them from the sin they have committed against me and will forgive all their sins of rebellion against me" (Jer. 33:8 NIV). Jesus died and shed His blood for us.

> "He did not enter by means of the blood of goats and calves; but He entered the Most Holy Place once for all by His own blood, having obtained eternal redemption ... In fact, the law requires that nearly everything be cleansed with blood, and without the shedding of blood there is no forgiveness." (Heb. 9:12, 22 NIV)

It is through the blood of Jesus that we are cleansed and forgiven of our sins. To receive that forgiveness, God says:

> "If we confess our sins, he is faithful and just and will forgive us our sins and purify us from all unrighteousness. If we claim we have not sinned, we make him out to be a liar and his word is not in us." (1 John 1:9-10 NIV)

Without repentance our sins are not forgiven, nor do we change our behavior. Repentance means we turn around and change. When we repent and ask God's forgiveness, we are cleansed, and God sees us as He sees Jesus in righteousness and purity. Some individuals have difficulty believing or asking God to forgive them. They may feel unworthy to receive His forgiveness. The truth is, none of us is worthy of God's forgiveness. It is by God's mercy—His unmerited favor and His love and grace toward us—that we can have forgiveness for our sins and a restored relationship with Him. None of us could stand before Father God if Jesus had not died on the cross for our sins and risen from the dead for our redemption. Since no one can do anything to obtain forgiveness and cleansing, God made a way for all to come to Him. We just need to come and believe that He is a rewarder of those who seek Him.

Many individuals can seek God's forgiveness on their own behalf, but struggle to forgive others who have caused them tremendous hurt and pain. A misunderstanding of what forgiveness is often hinders us from forgiving.

The following are some of the reasons we do not forgive:

1. We believe that if we forgive, then we have to trust the person who hurt us. Forgiveness is not the same as trust. We are commanded by God to forgive others if we want Jesus to forgive our sins. Trust grows in our heart when other people consistently prove by their actions and behavior that they are trustworthy. Trust has nothing to do with forgiveness.
2. We believe that if we forgive those who hurt us, then they are released from responsibility or punishment for their sin. Believing this means that those who hurt us are getting away with their sins. That is not true because God's Word says, "'It is mine to avenge; I will repay … The Lord will judge his people.' It is a dreadful thing to fall into the hands of the living God" (Heb. 10:30-31 NIV). Refusing to forgive hurts us, and it hurts others who know and love us. Our sin attitudes effect those around us. Not forgiving is hatred. Our offender does not feel our pain, but we will live with the pain and reap the consequences of unforgiveness.
3. We believe that the sin against us is too great to be forgiven. When we do not forgive, we are spiritually allowing the sins of our offender to be upon our shoulders. We carry the burden of their sin, and that is our sin. It is our mental attitude or physical body that suffers from the offense. Our relationship with God is hindered.
4. The offender does not take responsibility for the offense or keeps repeating it again and again. Forgiveness does not mean accepting or condoning unacceptable behavior. Ultimately, the offender will answer to God.

5. We feel people have deliberately hurt us, and they don't care what they did to us. God says to forgive so that He can forgive us.
6. We believe that we just cannot forgive. Forgiveness is *an act of the will* and *a miracle of grace.* God accomplishes it in us when we give Him our will. *Forgiveness is not a feeling.* We need to choose to forgive because God commands it. When we struggle with forgiving, we are in a spiritual battle with the enemy of our soul. It is Satan who promotes unforgiveness. We may need to bind and come against an unforgiving spirit if our struggle to forgive is intense.
7. We believe we are a hypocrite if we pray to forgive when we are angry with the person, don't like the person or don't feel like forgiving. Choosing to obey God's Word is walking in spiritual maturity. It is not being a hypocrite.
8. We excuse the person's offense because we think we understand why they offended. When this happens, we have displaced our anger and the sin offense onto someone or something else. We are not dealing with the real offense, but with the distortion of the offense. Forgiveness cannot take place unless we deal with "truth." The Word of God says, "Then you will know the truth, and the truth will set you free" (John 8:32 NIV).

> "For if you forgive other people when they sin against you, your heavenly Father will also forgive you. But if you do not forgive others their sins, your Father will not forgive your sins." (Matt. 6:14 NIV)

God clearly shows us in Matthew 18:21-35, that we are to forgive always. Jesus tells Peter that he is to forgive not seven times, but seventy times seven. In other words, we are to keep on forgiving. Jesus further shows that unforgiveness has consequences. The consequence is that we will be "tortured" until we forgive. Unforgiving people struggle with bitterness, resentment, no peace of mind, anger, rage, tormenting thoughts, hurtful memories, and physical problems. The price of unforgiveness is steep and produces only bad fruit in our lives.

Forgiveness Assignment

Write down the names of individuals who have hurt you or toward whom you have bitterness, resentment, anger or hatred.

If you have the above attitudes in your heart, you have not forgiven. Make a list identifying all the ways those people have hurt you.

After you clearly see what you need to forgive people for, make a list of your sinful attitudes, such as anger, desire to punish, hate, bitterness, revenge, etc.

Make a list of what you have done to others that you need to ask their forgiveness for.

After you have completed the above assignment, you need to choose to be obedient to God and pray through the above. The Word says, "Therefore confess your sins to each other and pray for each other so that you may be healed" (James 5:16 NIV). Find someone you can trust and pray with that person, confessing your sins and asking God's forgiveness as you forgive those whom have sinned against you.

Jesus, I forgive ________________________________ [*name the person who hurt you*] *for* ____

____

____

[*state all the hurtful incidents you* forgive him/her for]. *Lord, would you forgive* ________________________________ [name the person who hurt you]. *God, forgive me for holding* ____________________________

____

____

[name what is in your heart] *in my heart against the person. God, cleanse my heart from my sin and bless the one who has offended me. Thank You for doing it!*

Pray this prayer for each person who has offended or hurt you.

Write down what God has done in your heart, and praise Him for it.

Ask the Lord if He wants you to go to your offender and speak forgiveness to him/her. Sometimes God will request this of you, other times He will not. Seek His direction. If He does want you to go to that individual, ask for God's timing and what He wants you to say. Remember that Jesus always ministered to others from a heart of love and that is what He requires of you.

FOUNTAIN
of BLESSINGS and PROMISES from
GOD
ANGER
RESENTMENT
DECEIT
DISTRUST
UNFORGIVINGNESS
PRIDE
REJECTION
LONELY
UNWORTHINESS
UNLOVED
Hearts passion
for
GOD

JUDGMENTS

God tells us in His Word that we are not to judge others.

> "You, therefore, have no excuse, you who pass judgment on someone else, for at whatever point you judge another, you are condemning yourself, because you who pass judgment do the same things." (Rom. 2:1 NIV)

> "Do not judge, or you too will be judged. For in the same way you judge others, you will be judged, and with the measure you use, it will be measured to you. Why do you look at the speck of sawdust in your brother's eye and pay no attention to the plank in your own eye? How can you say to your brother, 'Let me take the speck out of your eye,' when all the time there is a plank in your own eye? You hypocrite, first take the plank out of your own eye, and then you will see clearly to remove the speck from your brother's eye." (Matt. 7:1-5 NIV)

As adults we usually have the intellectual and emotional maturity to recognize when we are judging another in our heart. If we are walking in obedience to the Lord and wanting our life to be right before Him, we will look at our sin of judgment and ask God's forgiveness. Judgments made as adults may not go as deep within our heart bringing deep pain and bondage as those made in childhood. This is because they can be easily and quickly identified and dealt with. However, the judgments we make when we are children go deep within the heart. As children we do not know what judgments are, nor do we have the spiritual or emotional maturity to know how to deal with judgments spiritually. When a child's spirit is wounded over and over again, that child will judge the one who hurt him or her. Judgments grow out of anger in the heart for what has happened.

Since a child does not know how to resolve the anger, the judgments go deep within the child's heart and may be hidden from the conscious mind for years.

> "See to it that no one falls short of the grace of God and that no bitter root grows up to cause trouble and defile many." (Heb. 12:15 NIV)

John Sanford says, "Those hidden roots of bitterness are judgments and angry responses made by us as children and then hidden from our conscious or unconscious mind; forgotten by us but very vivid and active in the subconscious. They are deep roots within our soul that feed into our life and we act upon them."[3] Because they are deep roots, they are hidden to our adult mind. The only evidence that the roots are there is our behaviors or belief system. Judgments in the soul produce bitterness, resentment, unforgiveness, and infect the mind with negative thinking. One may learn to expect the negative or worst to happen.

In his book *Transformation of the Inner Man,* John Sandford says, "bitterness in the heart infects the mind with negative psychological expectancies." He also states that "a bitter-root expectancy is a psychological practice built into our nature by which we expect and propel people to fulfill our pictures of the way life will go."[4] If these roots of bitterness are within the heart, relationships will be affected, and our mental attitude toward life will be warped.

The following are examples of bitter-root expectancies:

Example #1

A client came into my office complaining of the verbally abusive treatment she received from her husband. She was very angry and stated that she had always been treated badly by those who are supposed to love her. Then, she began to tell how her father used to call her very dirty, vile names. He had an order by which he said those things to her. What upset her so much was that her husband, who never knew her father or knew that her father called her those names, called her the same names and in the same order. When she asked God to forgive her for the judgment in her heart against her father and she forgave her father, she was released from the judgment and the bitter-root expectancy of being verbally abused. She then forgave her husband and the judgment she had in her heart toward him. God totally freed her from the sin of judgment and broke the cycle of belief that she would always be verbally abused.

God also dealt with the husband and his sinful responses. Healing took place in their relationship.

Example #2

A man who was raised by a very manipulative and controlling mother judged his mother for how she treated him. There was deep resentment in his heart toward her. Become of the judgments and anger in his heart toward his mother, he came to believe that all women manipulate and control. As a result, suggestions made by any woman, especially his wife, were seen as an attempt by the woman to control him. Because of his distorted belief system and his bitter-root expectancies, he had conflict in his relationships with women. He had to forgive his mother and ask God to forgive him for judging her, break the power of the bitter-root expectancy in his life and set him free. God freed him!

> "Do not be deceived: God cannot be mocked. A man reaps what he sows. Whoever sows to please their flesh, from the flesh will reap destruction; whoever sows to please the Spirit, from the Spirit will reap eternal life. Let us not become weary in doing good, for at the proper time we will reap a harvest if we do not give up." (Gal. 6:7-9 NIV)

If we allow judgments or bitter-root expectancies to be in operation in our life, we will reap the consequences of what we have sown. This is an unyielding law of God. God's grace is the only means by which we can obtain redemption for our sinful attitudes, thoughts and behaviors. The four fundamental laws in the Word of God are:

1. The law of honoring and dishonoring (Deut. 5:16).
2. The law of judging and receiving (Matt. 7:1).
3. The law of sowing and reaping (Gal. 6:7).
4. The law of becoming what we judge (Rom. 2:1).

Examples of Judgments

The law of judging and receiving: A young boy who was continually berated by his father and who judged his father now constantly reaps derogatory treatment from others.

The law of becoming what we judge: A woman who was continuously yelled at by her mother, judged her mother, and now yells and behaves just like her mother. A typical statement she might hear from others is: "You are just like your mother." When she hears this, it angers her. She may say rather venomously, "No, I am not!" Her behavioral response only confirms the judgments in her heart.

John and Paula Sandford teach that bitter-root judgment and expectancy are similar but not identical. "A person may have an expectancy pattern without having judged (for instance a positive expectancy to expect and draw respect from others)."[5] Most people can easily identify a bitter-root expectancy. However, judgments may have been made in earliest infancy and forgotten, thus causing us to develop behavior patterns in our life which seem unexplainable. We are often unaware why we feel or act the way we do because it happens so long after the sowing has been lost to awareness. For example, a woman may become involved in one abusive relationship after another when logically she wants to stay away from an abuser.

Bitter-root judgments do not deny free will. We have the freedom to choose whether or not to respond to bitter-root judgments or expectancies. But to do so, it would be like wading upstream against the current. Unless the grace of God intervenes, we will eventually follow our fleshly desires and intentions, giving in to the cycle of judgment and reap the consequences.

John and Paula Sandford teach that "a wife who had a violent father may turn a gentle husband into an abuser, either to herself and/or their children. Or a husband who had an abusive mother may turn a gentle wife into abusiveness, either to himself and/or their children. A wife whose mother was abusive may abuse, or a husband whose father was abusive may abuse, but that is caused by the operation of psychology and the law of judgment (Matt. 7:1), acting upon one's self, whereas daughter-father and son-mother sets up laws of bitter-root expectancy which act upon the mate."[6]

Diagnosis and Treatment

Bitter-root judgment and expectancy are very common and basic. In diagnosis, bitter-root judgment and expectancy are identified by recognizing and acknowledging the sinful attitudes and responses we have toward others and toward life, and tracking from that fruit to their roots in childhood.

> "For the word of God is alive and active. Sharper than any double-edged sword, it penetrates even to dividing soul and spirit, joints and marrow; it judges the thoughts and attitudes of the heart." (Heb. 4:12 NIV)

The Word of God is definite and incisive. It says that we will be known by our fruits (Matt. 7:16-20). If we have the bad fruit, we have the bad root. No matter what individuals protest about feelings or thoughts, fruits reveal roots! Treatment of bitter-roots, once seen and discussed, are healed by prayer.

Initial sins of judgment, bitterness and resentment are washed away only by the blood of Jesus Christ. The steps of forgiveness and cleansing are as follows:

1. One must first identify sinful attitudes and behaviors that are rooted in judgments.
2. One must choose to forgive the offender. In prayer the person needs to say:

   Jesus, I forgive ________________________ [name the person who hurt you] *for* ________________________
   ____
   ____
   ________________ [state what that person did to you]. *Lord, I ask that you forgive me for holding resentment and judgment* [or other sins you need to repent of] *in my heart against* ________________ [name the person who hurt you]. *God, cleanse me from this sin and set me free to have Christ-like godly attitudes. Bring my practice of bitter-root judgment and expectancy to death on Your cross, and give me a new and good expectancy.*

3. The person praying for you should pronounce forgiveness to you by the Word of the Lord. John 20:23 says, "If you forgive anyone's sins, their sins are forgiven; if you do not forgive them, they are not forgiven" (NIV). Your prayer partner should pray:

   Jesus, I come before you now and ask that You forgive ________________ [name the person you are praying for] *for the sins of judgment, resentment, bitterness, and anger that they held in their heart. I speak the forgiveness of Jesus Christ to* ________________________ [name the person you are praying for] *this day and pronounce their sins forgiven by the authority and blood of Jesus Christ. I command that all judgments and bitter-root expectancies be destroyed in their heart and mind by the cross of the Lord Jesus Christ. They are released and healed in the name of Jesus.*

> "I have been crucified with Christ and I no longer live, but Christ lives in me. The life I now live in the body, I live by faith in the Son of God, who loved me and gave himself for me." (Gal. 2:20 NIV)

Healing is finalized after we recognize the bitter-root judgments and expectancies we have made and bring them to the cross. God heals the heart through prayer.

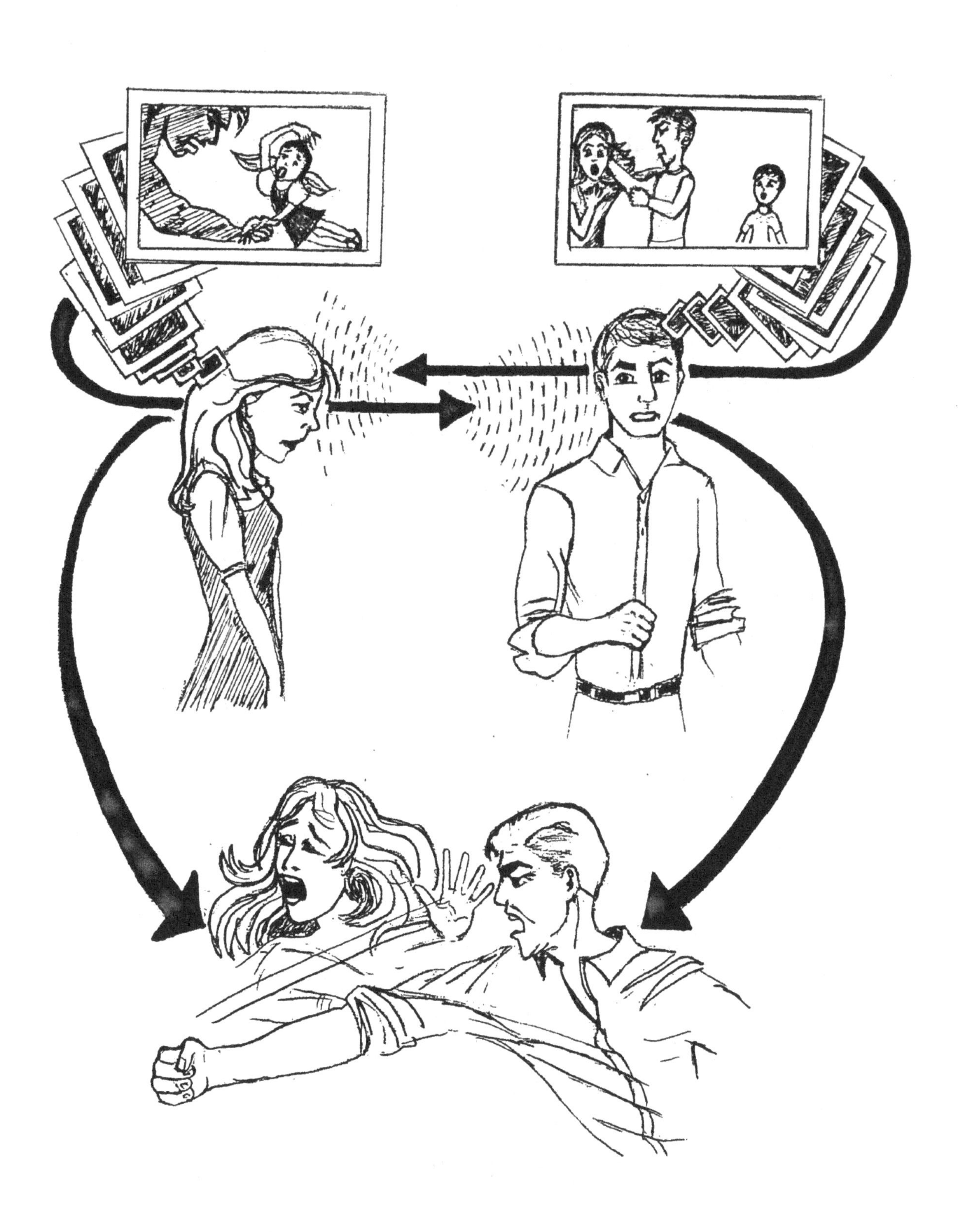

The following are examples of judgments made by several individuals who have been deeply wounded. These are given as an example to help you identify your judgments. Make your list of judgments and bitter-root expectancies. Then, pray through the judgments.

Examples of judgments against yourself

- I'm unlovable and ugly when I'm bigger than a size 7.
- I'm not nice.
- I'm desperately needy and will always fail at love.
- I am selfish and weak. No nobody will ever want me.

Examples of judgments women have against men

- Men are always demanding and have to have their own way.
- Men are unfaithful and lie all the time.
- Men avoid, sneak around and cheat.
- Men drop women at a drop of the hat if they don't get what they want.
- Men use women for sex and want women to take care of them and meet all their needs.
- Men are dogs.
- Men are manipulative, controlling and abusive emotionally, physically and sexually.
- Men expect women to look perfect.
- Men are only interested in sex.

Examples of judgments men have against women

- Women use me all the time.
- Women only want me when they need something.
- Women are deceitful and will stab me in the back.
- Women gossip all the time.
- Women are more concerned about themselves than others.
- Women are needy.
- Women will use me until they get what they want, and then they will leave me.
- All women are manipulative.
- Women want my money and are only interested in what I can get them.

- All women are bossy and controlling.
- Women lie and manipulate to control me.
- Women hate sex and will use it to frustrate me.
- Women are immoral.
- Women desire to be treated badly.

Bitter-Root Judgments and Expectancies Assignment

What are bitter-roots?

How do bitter-roots affect your heart?

What is bitter-root expectancy?

What are the four fundamental laws in the Word of God?

Explain Deuteronomy 5:16.

Explain Matthew 7:1-5.

Explain Galatians 6:7-8.

Explain Romans 2:1-3

Write down the bitter-root expectancies that you have and explain how they operate in your life.

Write down the judgments you have made toward men.

Write down the judgments you have made toward women.

Write down the judgments you have made toward God.

Write down the judgments you have made toward yourself.

How can you break these judgments?

Identify each step:

1.

2.

3.

What is the difference between a judgment and a bitter-root expectancy?

Explain how Matthew 7:16-20 relates to judgments and expectancies.

How do Galatians 2:20; 3:13 and 5:24 relate to judgments and expectancies?

Identify the individuals you need to forgive who have emotionally or physically wounded you or passed judgment on you.

Have you forgiven them? If not, what do you feel needs to happen for you to forgive them and release them to Jesus?

What does Jesus say will happen to you if you do not forgive?

HATRED
UNFORGIVENESS
RESENTFULNESS
BITTERNESS
YOU ARE RESPONSIBLE

Vows

Jesus has called us to have open and loving hearts toward others. When we have been deeply wounded, the natural and fleshly desire is to protect ourselves so that we do not get hurt again. One of the defense mechanisms to protect ourselves is to make a determination or a vow in our heart that will direct our thoughts, actions and behaviors.

> "Do not be quick with your mouth, do not be hasty in your heart to utter anything before God. God is in heaven and you are on earth, so let your words be few. A dream comes when there are many cares, and many words mark the speech of a fool. When you make a vow to God, do not delay to fulfill it. He has no pleasure in fools; fulfill your vow. It is better not to make a vow than to make one and not fulfill it. Do not let your mouth lead you into sin. And do not protest to the temple messenger, 'My vow was a mistake.' Why should God be angry at what you say and destroy the work of your hands?" (Eccles. 5:2-6 NIV)

To make a vow to the Lord is not sin, but to make a vow that is not rooted in sacrificial commitment to God is a sin. Vows that are made from a rebellious, stubborn, hardened, or stony heart have their root in sin. God says in Psalm 95:8, "Do not harden your hearts" (NIV). Vows are one detail of a stony heart. We are admonished by the Lord to lay aside the sins which so easily entangle us (Heb. 12:1) and put off the practices of our old nature (Col. 3:5-10). The inner vows we made as children will direct our heart, behavior and responses to others as adults. Rather than trust God to protect our heart, a sinful vow establishes us in fleshly control of our mind and emotions. Our flesh rules us rather than the Spirit of God.

John Sandford states an inner vow:[7]

- Is an unyielding structure controlled by the flesh and operating at an unconscious level for our emotional protection.
- Is a determination, a directive sent into our inner being, which controls our actions.
- Becomes a stubborn and powerful structure in our nature, whose specific function is to hold us to feel, think, and act out the vow.
- Refuses change. Vows are only broken by the power of prayer as we ask God to forgive us and break the stronghold of that vow in our life.

The majority of vows we make are made during childhood. To break a vow, we must first identify past childhood hurts and how we responded to those hurts. We identify the vows we have made by recognizing what we said that we would or would not do in our life as a result of those hurts.

Examples

- I will never cry again if someone hurts me.
- No one will ever tell me what to do.
- I'll get even with him if it's the last thing I ever do.
- No one will ever know my heart or how I feel.
- I will never trust anyone again.
- I will not submit to those in authority.

To break vows, we must first:

1. Recognize the vows we have made.
2. Repent of the sinful responses which caused us to make each vow (hate, resentment, vengeance, etc...)
3. Ask God to forgive us for making the vow.
4. Forgive those who hurt us.
5. Take authority—sinful vows can only be broken by our authority in Christ (Matt. 18:18). Command the vow (naming it) to be broken by the power of the cross and the blood of Jesus.
6. Ask God to replace that vow with His love and the truth of His Word.

7. Determine to overcome our sinful habit by prayer and praise to God for our deliverance.
8. Set our heart to respond to others in love and compassion.

Example #1

A woman who had been badly berated, shamed and controlled by her father when she was young made a vow that "no man would ever tell her what to do." Years later, when she got married, her heart would not receive input or advice from her husband. She was not able to see his concern and advice as godly love and protection. Instead, she saw him as trying to control her. When she broke the vow, her heart was open to her husband, and she could receive from him.

Example #2

A man who was raised with a mother who was very manipulative and controlling said, "No woman is ever going to tell me what to do." As a married man, he had difficulty accepting suggestions from his wife. He saw her suggestions as trying to control him. This produced a lot of conflict in their marriage. When he broke the vow, he was able to accept his wife's input in a positive way. The result was less conflict between them.

Remember that inner vows are the result of woundedness and angry responses made when we were children. They were stated in the mind, whether consciously or unconsciously, and then sent directly to the heart. We can and do make vows as adults, but those vows seldom have the power and impact upon us as those made during childhood. Any inner vow that prevents us from responding in a godly way is rooted in sin and needs to be broken by the power of the cross and the name of Jesus.

Vows Assignment

Go back over the journaling you have done and begin to identify any inner vows that you made when you were hurt. If you have a hard time recognizing the vows, write down what you believe about women, men, life, God, or yourself. Your belief system will help you recognize the vows that control your heart. Then pray together with someone for the vows to be broken and your heart cleansed from your sinfulness. Pray:

> *Lord Jesus, I ask you to forgive me for making the vow to* ____________________ [state the vow]. *I command that the power and sin of this vow be broken in my heart and mind by the power of the cross of Jesus Christ. I ask, Lord, that You "create in me a pure heart, Oh God, and renew a steadfast spirit within me"* (Ps. 51:10 NIV). *Thank You, Jesus, for breaking this vow and cleansing me from this sin. I forgive* ________________________________ [name the individuals] *who have wounded me that resulted in my making this vow.*
>
> "Direct my footsteps according to your word; let no sin rule over me." (Ps. 119:133 NIV)
>
> "Set a guard over my mouth, Lord; keep watch over the door of my lips. Let not my heart be drawn to what is evil, to take part in wicked deeds." (Ps. 141:3-4 NIV)

INNER
VOWS

INNER
VOWS

Belief Systems and Strongholds

Is our identity in Christ or in the lies Satan has given us?

Who is Satan? He is the father of all liars. Lies are Satan's plans to throw off our identity and bring us into deception. Satan does not want us to believe and to apply to our lives what God says about us. Satan wants to leave us powerless, so he deceives us into believing lies.

> "He [Satan] was a murderer from the beginning, not holding to the truth, for there is no truth in him. When he lies, he speaks his native language, for he is a liar and the father of lies." (John 8:44-45 NIV)

(See the assignment at the end of this section to identify lies you may believe about yourself or others.)

Rejection was what Satan brought to earth when he was kicked out of heaven because of his pride and rebellion. Satan built upon the rejection by causing distrust to develop in our heart. When our trust has been broken, it is easy to believe lies about ourselves, others and God.

Four major lies are rooted in fear and shame:

1. <u>Fear of Failure</u>: The fear of failure can cause us to strive continually to obtain perfection so that we feel worthy. We also may not try at all due to fear of failure.
2. <u>Fear of Rejection</u>: We need to be approved by others in order to feel accepted. Feelings of rejection can cause us to seek approval from others in very dysfunctional and unhealthy ways. People who do this are always looking to others to make them feel better. If they don't receive the approval needed, it reinforces the lie that others will always reject them.

3. Fear of Punishment: We'd rather blame others or ourselves than be punished or feel guilt. Being sarcastic, critical and harsh toward others often manifests this. We may enter into excessively explaining ourselves to avoid blame/criticism or shame. Fear of punishment may cause us to feel like we need to be perfect. There is no perfect person. When an individual cannot obtain perfection, they may give up on life. They believe they are hopeless or worthless.
4. Presence of Shame, Hopelessness and Helplessness: We feel doomed, defective and unable to change. That belief system will often lead us into believing we are worthless, bad, and unacceptable. Life will never be any different for us so why try.

Satan's Lie: Our performance combined with other people's opinions = our self-worth.

God's Truth: We are perfect in Christ, children of God, the temple of the Holy Spirit, with enough power to do whatever God wants us to do (Col. 1:9-14).

The Truth of God's Word in Operation in Us
= Our True Identity and Value

Jesus died so that we could obtain victory over all the lies of Satan. Jesus did that through:

- **Justification:** Means we are forgiven; innocent of all wrong; free from all blame; declared guiltless; absolved; acquitted. In God's eyes, it is "just as if" we never sinned. Fear of failure can be eliminated and brought to death in our life if we understand and accept God's justification for our sins.
- **Reconciliation:** The work of Christ that opposes rejection. Meaning, we are fully approved/accepted by God unconditionally. He receives us as we are. (John 15:16; Col. 1:21-22; Rom. 5:9-12; 2 Cor. 5:17-21)
- **Atonement:** Christ has resolved God's perfect justice for us. We are no longer under God's punishment. Jesus' blood turns away God's wrath. We are not under punishment since we are in Christ. Satan tries to tell us we will be punished, but it is a LIE. God's mercy = unmerited favor. (Eph. 2:4-10; Rom. 3:25-26; 1 John 4:9-10; Heb. 2:17; Rom. 8:1; Gal. 3:13)
- **Regeneration:** We are new beings in Christ. To be regenerated means to be renewed; restored; made better, especially after a decline to a low or abject

condition. To be reborn. Shame and hopelessness no longer have any power over us. We become new creations in Christ. (2 Cor. 5:17; Titus 3:5-6; 1 Pet. 1:3-5)

The tactics and approach Satan uses to bring us into bondage frequently work in the following ways:

- Rejection comes to us through wounding.
- Lies enter our heart.
- Deception comes and brings strongholds in our life.

What is a stronghold? It is a place having strong defenses; fortified place; fortress; secure refuge. There can be individual or generational strongholds.

An individual mental stronghold is much more than a habit. It is a strong fleshly control within us that is rooted in such sins as selfishness, rebellion, pride, rejection and shame. The stronghold controls our thoughts and emotions. The function of the stronghold is to keep truth from penetrating our inner man, which keeps us from repentance, forgiveness and freedom. A stronghold blinds us from the truth and, therefore, keeps us in bondage to the sins of the flesh. This prevents our mind from understanding and seeing the deception put upon us by Satan. Our mind does not recognize and receive (take hold of) attitudes or behaviors that may be wrong.

At the core, each stronghold contains lies. When the truth of God's Word tries to penetrate the stronghold, demons of deception try to reinforce the stronghold with more lies and false feelings. The goal of the enemy is to prevent truth from being received, keeping the walls of defense fortified and the person in bondage. The function of an individual mental stronghold is to keep the person from thinking effectively, repenting, and praying against the stronghold to destroy the sinful thoughts and fleshly behaviors.

Means of defilement that allow demonic entry:

- Unforgiveness
- Hatred/bitterness
- Lack of resistance to sinful fleshly thoughts or behaviors
- Lack of resistance to Satan's attacks

The sins Satan finds most potent are:

- Bitter-root judgments and expectancies

- Unforgiveness
- Unrepentance
- Inner vows

These are trusted defenses of the flesh, but they do not work toward victory. They produce further bondage and open us up to more attacks from the enemy. Other false defenses that can be used for self-protection are denial, avoidance of pain and hurt, dissociation, projection, repression, and displacement.

Intrapsychic is data and concepts representing processes that take place beneath the level of awareness (i.e. in the unconscious).

The following are definitions of each defense mechanism:

- **Denial:** A group of intrapsychic processes that enable hurting people to prevent intolerable thoughts, perceptions or inklings from rising to consciousness. People that use denial do not see the problem.
- **Avoidance:** A strategy designed by an individual to avoid pain, to need nothing, to depend on no one and to deny desires. The person turns from him/herself and others.
- **Dissociation:** A neurotic syndrome in which normally associated segments of memory and thought are split off from each other.
- **Projection:** An intrapsychic mechanism in which the person denies his/her own unacceptable traits and impulses, and ascribes them to others.
- **Repression:** An intrapsychic mechanism in which painful memories and impulses are pushed down and kept from consciousness.
- **Displacement:** An intrapsychic mechanism by which emotions are transferred from their original object to a seemingly more acceptable substitute.

God has given mankind a tremendous mind. A child who experiences intense pain, rejection or abandonment develops ways to cope with life. Such children use many defense mechanisms to protect themselves. They also “fill in the blanks” in their heart and mind where they do not have understanding of situations or emotional wholeness. Coming into wholeness involves identifying the above coping mechanisms and appropriating God’s truth within the heart and mind. If this does not happen, Satan continues to enjoy a playfield of lies and strongholds.

Satan is the father of lies (John 8:44). A lying spirit helps one become more adept at covering up lies, and that leads to compulsive lying. Each time we lie, the practice in the flesh and the demon using it become stronger. Lies grow out of a lifelong feeling of POWERLESSNESS. That is where Satan fortifies his house and holds a person in bondage.

Listed below are areas that may be strongholds in our life:

Hate	Pride
Unforgiveness	Suspicion
Revenge	Murder
Bitterness	Guilt
Self-Hatred	Rebellion
Resentment	Fear
Anger	Depression
Self-Rejection	Self-Pity
Jealousy	Independence
Stubbornness	Low Self-Esteem
Defensiveness	Sexual Immorality
Sexual Perversions	Self-Destruction
Excessive Need to Compete	Lying
Stealing	Self-Centeredness
Control	Addictive Behavior

Satan brings the following six strongholds against people in an attempt to destroy who they are in Christ:

- Self-Hatred
- Self-Pity
- Self-Destruction
- Low Self-Esteem
- Self-Rejection
- Self-Centeredness

If we accept any of these strongholds, we will struggle in every area of our walk with the Lord. We will be unable to know and comprehend who we are in Christ and lack understanding of our value and purpose as children of God. Breaking these strongholds is vital in order to have a victorious walk in Christ, maintain peace of mind, and understand the loving heart of Father God.

Distrust within the heart results when we close our heart off to others and allow Satan to further reinforce the belief that others cannot be trusted. Allowing distrust leaves our heart vulnerable for more rejection. Distrust further states, "God, I do not trust you with my life." This puts us in the position of calling God a liar.

> "Blessed be the God and Father of our Lord Jesus Christ, who hath blessed us with all spiritual blessings in heavenly places in Christ; according as He hath *chosen* us in Him before the foundation of the world, that we should be *holy and without blame* before Him in love, having predestinated us to adoption of children by Jesus Christ to Himself, according to the good pleasure of His will, to the praise of the glory of His grace, *Wherein He hath made us accepted in the Beloved.*" (Eph. 1:3-6 NKJV)

God accepts us even while we still have bad fruit in our life. God says He is "changing us from glory to glory." Our job is to allow God to do the work that He desires to do in our lives. Resisting the work of the Holy Spirit often stems from the belief that God will reject us because we cannot measure up to His expectations, or we are unworthy of receiving any blessings from God. The *spirit of rejection* attacks us in four ways:

1. The spirit of rejection comes against us when we are wounded.
2. We feel or envision rejection from others.
3. We reject ourselves before others can reject us.
4. We desire rejection. Rejection is what is familiar. We have lived with rejection for so long that we anticipate and accept rejection.

Satan uses rejection to defeat us. His key weapon is deception. He deceives us by causing us to believe untruth. With deception comes false guilt and fear.

False guilt prevents one who has been accepted in Christ from receiving His acceptance. Satan uses the lie of guilt to keep people from walking in freedom. The Word says, "Therefore, there is now no condemnation [guilt] for those who are in Christ Jesus" (Rom. 8:1 NIV). True guilt drives us to conviction about our sin, produces repentance, builds our faith, and causes us to walk in regeneration.

Fear underlies all rejection. It produces the expectation that we will be rejected again and again. It can become a self-fulfilling prophecy in our life if we do not come against the work of Satan. Rejection fuels perfectionism and procrastination. Behind these behaviors is a fear of failure. Fear of failure is powerful because the underlying belief is that others will reject us or we will reject ourselves. Consequently, a mindset is developed that says, "I will do everything myself." Perfectionism is overcompensation to avoid the pain of rejection. It results in self-defeating behavior. Procrastination is avoidance through inaction. We avoid completing a task because that might result in conflict, loss of approval, or failure because of fear of rejection. God says, "There is no fear in love; but perfect love casts out fear, because fear involves torment" (1 John 4:18 NKJV).

> "Peace I leave with you, my peace give I unto you; not as the world giveth, give I unto you. Let not your heart be troubled, neither let it be afraid." (John 14:27 KJV)

To overcome all that Satan has put into our lives, we must identify the enemy, his weapons, and how to counter-attack him to win the battle.

The enemy is:	Satan
The battleground is:	Our mind, emotions and will
Satan's weapons are:	Deception, rejection, lies, distrust, and fear
Our weapons are:	The Word of God, the blood of Jesus, the name of Jesus, and the word of our testimony

To battle the enemy effectively, we must understand how to use the weapons God has given us. Jesus defeated Satan by using the Word of God.

In Matthew 4:4, Jesus says, "It is written: 'Man shall not live on bread alone, but on every word that comes from the mouth of God'" (NIV). When we battle the enemy, we are to quote the Word of God to him.

When Jesus died on the cross, He shed His blood for the remission of sin. It is through the blood of Jesus that we have power to come against the works of Satan and to come into healing.

> "Surely he took up our pain and bore our suffering, yet we considered him punished by God, stricken by him, and afflicted. But he was pierced for our transgressions, he was crushed for our iniquities; the punishment that brought us peace was on him, and by his wounds we are healed. We all, like sheep, have gone astray, each of us has turned to our own way; and the Lord has laid on him the iniquity of us all." (Isaiah 53:4-6 NIV)

When Jesus was beaten, crucified, and then rose from the dead, He defeated all that hell intended for us. He took all of our sin upon Himself and promised us victory in our life if we pray using the name of Jesus and the power of the blood, which He shed for us. Satan cannot stand against the name of Jesus or the power of His blood. Just one drop of Jesus' blood is enough to accomplish all that we need.

Revelation 12:11 says, "And they overcame him by the blood of the Lamb and by the word of their testimony, and they did not love their lives to the death" (NKJV). As we speak the words of God and testify to His love and power, we defeat the works of Satan. Satan cannot stand against what God has done. What God has done in our life cannot be disputed by others or by the enemy of our soul.

We need to use the weapons that God has given to us, and we will walk in victory. "For our struggle is not against flesh and blood, but against the rulers, against the authorities, against the powers of this dark world and against the spiritual forces of evil in the heavenly realms" (Eph. 6:12 NIV).

To obtain victory, we must:

1. Identify the wound that originally entered our heart that gave Satan a foothold in the mind and emotions.
2. Ask God to show us what is in our heart toward those who have wounded us. Come against any binding or blocking spirit that may hinder us from doing what God asks us to do.
3. Choose to forgive those who have hurt us, forgive ourselves, and forgive God. Forgiveness is an act of our will, not a feeling.
4. Take authority in Christ and command that the stronghold be broken and all lies be put to death by the power of the cross.
5. Apply God's Word to every lie that Satan brings our way. Repeat appropriate scripture verses until we are walking in total freedom.
6. Choose to open our heart and be vulnerable to others, trusting that God will protect, guide and direct us.
7. Praise God daily for what He is doing in our life.
8. Spend time with individuals who will edify and build us up. If we keep company with those who may have the same strongholds, we may be pulled back into our old patterns of behavior and the strongholds will once again have a foothold in our life.

Belief System and Strongholds Assignment

Check the lies you believe and then write down what happened to you that resulted in your believing the lie.

Identify any lies you believe about yourself that may not be on the list below.

Journal about that woundedness, and then have someone pray with you to be released from those lies.

- Command all lies to be broken by the power of the cross and the blood of Jesus.
- Pray that the strongholds that maintain the lies be pulled down and their structures in your life be destroyed.

The following is a list of lies people believe. Check the ones you have believed or occasionally thought about yourself.

- ☐ Nothing I say or do is right.
- ☐ Why try? I always do things wrong.
- ☐ I never do anything right.
- ☐ I'll never be any good.
- ☐ I am trouble.
- ☐ I have to do things perfect.
- ☐ I can't win no matter what.
- ☐ I am a nobody.
- ☐ I am crazy.
- ☐ Life is bad, unhappy, no good.
- ☐ I am damaged goods.
- ☐ No one loves me.
- ☐ I am a fool.
- ☐ I don't have any power.
- ☐ I am stupid.
- ☐ I am not lovable.
- ☐ Something is wrong with me.
- ☐ I should not exist.
- ☐ It is better to be alone; people will hurt me.
- ☐ I am fat, nobody will ever love me.
- ☐ I am not worth listening to.
- ☐ I am unacceptable.

- ☐ I am hard to love.
- ☐ It is not okay to ask for help.
- ☐ I should have been a boy and/or I should have been a girl.
- ☐ I am like a prostitute.
- ☐ I make people abuse me.
- ☐ I feel like a liar, but I know I'm not a liar.
- ☐ I am too much to love.
- ☐ I am different from everyone else.
- ☐ I am hopeless.
- ☐ I am bad or naughty
- ☐ I am not important.
- ☐ I am unwanted.
- ☐ I can't achieve.
- ☐ I am not smart.
- ☐ I can't rely on anyone but myself.
- ☐ I am nothing.
- ☐ I feel like I don't really exist.
- ☐ I am just here to meet other peoples' needs.
- ☐ I am a failure.
- ☐ If I am honest, I will get hurt.
- ☐ I am not worthy of being blessed.
- ☐ Life will not go well for me.
- ☐ I can't stand up to evil.
- ☐ I should not exist.
- ☐ I am a non-person.
- ☐ I'm unworthy of any respect.
- ☐ I will always be abandoned.

WOUNDS	BELIEFS	BEHAVIORS	STRONGHOLDS	HEALING
Rejected and lied to as child by parents	I must perform to be accepted. I feel unloved.	Drugs & alcohol abuse	A mind set … purpose to prevent you from seeing the problem	Identify wounds received because of learning disability
Deceived	I have nothing to contribute. I don't love me.	Set self up for rejection	Fear of rejection	Acknowledge rejection by parents
Emotionally neglected	I can't deal with problems.	Lawlessness, rebellious	Powerlessness	Break generational sin of perversion and suicide
Family perversions	I am always wrong, bad, a failure/weak, powerless, hopeless, unworthy to be blessed.	Failed in school, sports, math; so wouldn't pursue	Fear of failure	Repent and break rebellion and lawless behavior
Dyslexia; shamed, made to feel inadequate	Attacks against the mind	Do things at last minute	Suicide	Renew mind with the Word of God
Powerless	Fantasize of being seduced by a woman	Not able to deal with problems until under pressure	Lawlessness	Be obedient to God's Word
Stupid	Thoughts of being propositioned, but no desire for a man	Lack of responsibility; none given as child; Argumentative; I'm right	Generational sin of perversion	
Brother's suicide	Perversion; thoughts of rape, but wouldn't do; porno given at age 10; feelings of fear, confusion and torment	Anger, rage, passivity, selflessness; meet own needs; memory blockage; controlling; fear of confrontation		

WOUNDS	BELIEFS	BEHAVIORS	STRONGHOLDS	HEALING

Defeating Sinful Thoughts, Behaviors and Pride

Jesus clearly says in His Word that the enemy will attack us, but we can overcome him by the word of our testimony, the blood of Jesus, and the Word of God (Rev. 12:11). Many times we fall short of being what God has called us to be because we do not know how to recognize the work of Satan and what steps we need to take to defeat him and his plans for us.

According to 1 John 2:15-16, Satan entices us in three ways:

1. The Lust of the Flesh
2. The Lust of the Eyes
3. The Pride of Life

The Lust of the Flesh

The lust of the flesh is defined as animal appetites, cravings, passions (Gen. 3:6). Lust is anything that controls us.

Lust will draw us into meeting the needs of our flesh without considering the consequences of our actions or behaviors. Our flesh controls us rather than our spirit.

Lust draws us away from the will of God (Gal. 5:16). Lust destroys our dependence upon God (John 15:5).

> "So I say, walk by the Spirit, and you will not gratify the desires of the flesh. For the flesh desires what is contrary to the Spirit, and the Spirit what is contrary to the flesh. They are in conflict with each other, so that you are not to do whatever you want." (Gal. 5:16-17 NIV)

These acts of the sinful nature are not broken by prayer for deliverance, but by submitting to God, disciplining the flesh, and walking in willful obedience to the Lord.

> "When tempted, no one should say, 'God is tempting me.' For God cannot be tempted by evil, nor does he tempt anyone; but each person is tempted when they are dragged away by their own evil desire and enticed. Then, after desire has conceived, it gives birth to sin; and sin, when it is full-grown, gives birth to death." (James 1:13-15 NIV)

The following are acts of the sinful nature that need to be brought to death, or we will not inherit the kingdom of God (Gal. 5):

CAROUSING	ARROGANCE	DIVISIONS
IMMORALITY	IMPURITY	IDOLATRY
SENSUALITY	SORCERY	ENMITIES
STRIFE	JEALOUSY	DISPUTES
DISSENSIONS	FACTIONS	ENVYING
DRUNKENNESS	PRIDE	OUTBURSTS OF ANGER

> "The mind governed by the flesh is death, but the mind governed by the Spirit is life and peace. The mind governed by the flesh is hostile to God; it does not submit to God's law, nor can it do so. Those who are in the realm of the flesh cannot please God." (Rom. 8:6-8 NIV)

> "For if you live according to the flesh, you will die; but if by the Spirit you put to death the misdeeds of the body, you will live." (Rom. 8:13 NIV)

The Lust of the Eyes

The lust of the eyes is defined as selfishness, self-interest, eye catching, enticing. Again, when lust seeks to control, it will entice us into all kinds of sin. It will draw us away from the Word of God (Matt. 16:24). It will destroy our confidence in God (John 15:7).

Genesis 3:6-7 says this about Eve:

> "When the woman saw that the fruit of the tree was good for food and pleasing to the eye, and also desirable for gaining wisdom, she took some

> and ate it. She also gave some to her husband, who was with her, and he ate it. Then the eyes of both of them were opened, and they realized they were naked; so they sewed fig leaves together and made coverings for themselves." (NIV)

Satan caused the fruit on the tree to appear pleasing to the eyes of Eve. The loveliness of the fruit tempted her to believe what Satan was telling her. "'You will not certainly die,' the serpent said to the woman. 'For God knows that when you eat from it your eyes will be opened, and you will be like God, knowing good and evil'" (Gen. 3:4-5 NIV). Eve listened to Satan. Adam disobeyed God and listened to Eve and Satan. That was their downfall and the beginning of the pathway of sin for all mankind. Mankind has battled the sin of the lust of the eyes ever since. Lustful eyes has been the downfall of many men and women. The lust of the eye can include many areas of sin. Some of these include:

- Desire for wealth.
- Desire for sexual encounters outside biblical guidelines.
- Desire for material things. (Examples: The best cars, boats, trucks, home, clothes.)
- Desire to be the best or the first in whatever we do.
- Worldly influence becomes too important to our self-esteem.
- Grandiose ideas about ourselves or our future.

A godly person needs to learn to submit to God and not to earthly possessions or desires.

> "Do not love the world or anything in the world. If anyone loves the world, love for the Father is not in them. For everything in the world—the lust of the flesh, the lust of the eyes, and the pride of life—comes not from the Father but from the world." (1 John 2:15-16 NIV)

> "Therefore do not let sin reign in your mortal body so that you obey its evil desires. Do not offer any part of yourself to sin as an instrument of wickedness, but rather offer yourselves to God as those who have been brought from death to life; and offer every part of yourself to him as an instrument of righteousness. For sin shall no longer be your master, because you are not under the law, but under grace. What then? Shall

> we sin because we are not under the law but under grace? By no means! Don't you know that when you offer yourselves to someone as obedient slaves, you are slaves of the one you obey—whether you are slaves to sin, which leads to death, or to obedience, which leads to righteousness?" (Rom. 6:12-16 NIV)

Pride of Life

Pride of life is defined as self-promotion, self-exaltation, haughtiness.

> "The Lord detests all the proud of heart. Be sure of this: They will not go unpunished." (Prov. 16:5 NIV)

> "Pride goes before destruction, a haughty spirit before a fall." (Prov. 16:18 NIV)

> "Pride brings a man low, but the lowly in spirit gain honor." (Prov. 29:23 NIV)

One of the major attitudes in our heart that prevents us from being victorious and Christ-like is pride. Satan was kicked out of heaven because he was proud and wanted to rule in place of God the Father. When Satan was rejected from heaven, the three major strongholds he brought to earth were rejection, rebellion and pride. Pride represents the underlying foundation for all sin. All disobedience, rebellion and foolishness find their roots in pride.

One of the saddest examples of what pride can do is told in the story of Nebuchadnezzar in Daniel 4. Nebuchadnezzar knew God and His power but chose to exalt himself rather than God. God warned Nebuchadnezzar in a dream what would happen to him if he did not change. Daniel interpreted the dream and told him, "Renounce your sins by doing what is right, and your wickedness by being kind to the oppressed. It may be that then your prosperity will continue" (Daniel 4:27 NIV). The story continues as follows:

> All this happened to King Nebuchadnezzar. Twelve months later, as the king was walking on the roof of the royal palace of Babylon, he said, "Is not this the great Babylon I have built as the royal residence, by my mighty power, and for the glory of my majesty?"

> The words were still on his lips when a voice came from heaven, "This is what is decreed for you, King Nebuchadnezzar, your royal authority has been taken from you. You will be driven away from people and will live with the wild animals; you will eat grass like cattle. Seven times will pass by for you until you acknowledge that the Most High is sovereign over the kingdoms of men and gives them to anyone he wishes."
>
> Immediately what had been said about Nebuchadnezzar was fulfilled. He was driven away from people and ate grass like cattle. His body was drenched with the dew of heaven until his hair grew like the feathers of an eagle and his nails like the claws of a bird.
>
> "At the end of that time, I Nebuchadnezzar, raised my eyes toward heaven, and my sanity was restored. Then I praised the Most High; I honored and glorified Him who lives forever ... Now I, Nebuchadnezzar, praise and exalt and glorify the King of heaven, because everything He does is right and all His ways are just. And those who walk in pride He is able to humble." (Daniel 4:28-34, 37 NIV)

Our pride prevents us from learning from our mistakes, disappointments and life difficulties. We often become fools and make choices in life we deeply regret. When they are going through difficulties, many individuals want other people's help, sympathy and understanding, but are unwilling to look at what sins in their own life may be contributing to their problems. Oftentimes because of pride, we want to be rescued out of our troubles rather than face our sins and allow God to change us. Difficult situations could be resolved with deep healing and restoration in our heart if we would look at what part pride plays in our problems.

Overcoming pride is the key to gaining victory and understanding when life has disappointed us. If Nebuchadnezzar had dealt with his pride, he would not have lost his kingship, his health, his friends, and his relationship with God. God hates pride, and He will deal with that sin in our life if we will not recognize and deal with it. Pride can only lead to our destruction and the downfall of others.

The following is a list of symptoms that I describe in my own words based upon Floyd McClung, Jr.'s book, *The Father Heart of God*:[8]

- Pride sees the wrongs of others but never identifies with their weaknesses. Without pride, we can respond, "Yes, I've done that too," or "I understand. If it were not for God's grace, I would have done that also."
- Pride does not usually admit wrong or personal responsibility. When it does, it excuses it or explains it away, and there is no sorrow for the wrong done.
- Pride blames others, criticizing and pointing out why they are wrong.
- Pride produces harshness, arrogance, self-sufficiency, and unhealthy independence.
- Pride causes us to seek acceptance in the eyes of other people more than being right according to God's standards.
- Pride is more concerned with winning an argument than how the other person is feeling.
- Pride never says the words, "I am wrong. It is my fault. Will you forgive me?"
- Pride breeds a demanding attitude. It focuses on what has not been done for us rather than on what has been done for us. It covets the past or the future but is never satisfied with the present.
- Pride is divisive. Pride says that "my way of thinking is what is right and you are wrong."
- Pride causes a person to judge situations by what they mean to man rather than to God. Pride does not look for God's perspective.
- Pride gossips, tears down, ruins reputations, and delights in spreading news of failure and sin. Pride blames God and other people when things go wrong.
- Pride excuses bitterness and resentment.
- Pride leads to self-pity. A "poor me" attitude.
- Pride says that a person can reach or has reached depth of spirituality in which we are finally free of pride. It puts its security in a grotesque form of self-righteousness and not in the cross of Jesus Christ.

David was a "man after God's own heart" because he humbled himself again and again. Psalm 51:17 says, "The sacrifice acceptable to God is a broken spirit; a broken and contrite heart, Oh God, thou wilt not despise" (KJV).

To David, brokenness did not mean hurt, despair or hopelessness. It was humility, which is the opposite of pride. Because of David's heart response, he learned from every disappointment in life, and God exalted him and raised him to kingship. When things go wrong, we can either look for God's reasons or become hard, rebellious and proud. David saw God in all of his circumstances.

There is no middle ground for a Christian. A mixture of humility and pride will not bring the results God desires. Even if we have done nothing wrong, we still need to learn to forgive and bless our enemies. That can only happen when we humble ourselves.

David was a humble man, but his predecessor was not. Saul was proud and did not have a heart of repentance for his sins. If we have a "Saulish" heart, we will reap destruction in our lives and the blessings of the Lord will not be released to us. Saul had such deep insecurities that he perceived others as a threat to himself personally and to the nation. His pride produced rebellion, and he ultimately walked out of God's blessing and hand of provision. The result was that he lost his kingdom, his son, and his life. Pride will only lead to destruction in anyone's life.

Individuals who are proud are also foolish. They do not clearly see their own sins or weakness. If they do recognize their sinful attitudes or behaviors, they may minimize or excuse them. Oftentimes they function from a rebellious heart rooted in witchcraft and wickedness.

Pride prevents Christians from entering into the deeper realms of the Spirit of God. Pride deceives us into thinking we are doing things for God, whereas we are really doing things for ourselves to make us look good to self and others. Pride leads us to respond with an "I," "me," or "mine" attitude. If what we do is not based on love for the Lord or for another person, our attitudes or responses are rooted in pride. Jesus clearly teaches us in His Word that we are to be humble and willing to be a servant to others. Jesus washed the feet of His disciples and told them they should do the same for others.

> "Now that I, your Lord and Teacher, have washed your feet, you also should wash one another's feet. I have set you an example that you should do as I have done for you. Very truly I tell you, no servant is greater than his master, nor is a messenger greater than the one who sent him. Now that you know these things, you will be blessed if you do them." (John 13:14-17 NIV)

Jesus calls us to humility and servanthood. Any attitude or behavior less than that is sin, and we will reap the consequences. Pride makes us foolish and brings shame. Pride also produces rebellion which brings destruction. Those sins produce wickedness. Wickedness is conscious intentional sin. Let us walk in righteousness and not reap the consequences of wickedness.

Remember that Satan frequently comes to us by asking us a question. In response to the question, he wants us to blame others for our failure. In Genesis 3:1, the serpent asked Eve, "Did God really say, 'You must not eat from any tree in the garden'?" (NIV). Adam blamed Eve when God questioned him, and Eve blamed the serpent.

> "And he said, 'Who told you that you were naked? Have you eaten from the tree that I commanded you not to eat from?' The man said, 'The woman you put here with me—she gave me some fruit from the tree, and I ate it.' Then the Lord God said to the woman, 'What is this you have done?' The woman said, 'The serpent deceived me, and I ate.'" (Gen. 3:11-13 NIV)

We must take responsibility for our own sins. Our fleshly lusts wage war against the soul. When we walk the ways of the world, indulging in fleshly desires, we are living according to the dictates of the prince of the air, the spirit who works in the sons of disobedience. We are indulging in the desires of our flesh and our mind, and we have become one with the nature of children of wrath (Eph. 2:3-4).

> "What causes fights and quarrels among you? Don't they come from your desires that battle within you? You desire but do not have, so you kill. You covet but you cannot get what you want, so you quarrel and fight. You do not have because you do not ask God. When you ask, you do not receive, because you ask with wrong motives, that you may spend what you get on your pleasures. You adulterous people, don't you know that friendship with the world means enmity against God? Therefore, anyone who chooses to be a friend of the world becomes an enemy of God." (James 4:1-4 NIV)

Jesus has given us every tool we need to overcome our flesh, the lust of the eyes, and pride. We need to know how to use the tools and be faithful and obedient in using them. If we are, victory will be ours. If we lay down our weapons, the enemy wins, and we become defeated spiritually, emotionally, physically, financially, and relationally. The home is Satan's number one target. If he destroys a husband and wife's relationship, he destroys the home and targets the children for destruction. To destroy Satan's plans and keep us free from demons, we must KEEP OUR LIFE FULL OF THE WORD OF GOD BY:

- Being in the Word every day.
- Praying daily.
- Fasting.

These are not mere lifestyle "rules" for the Christian walk. These are fundamental requirements for a successful relationship with God. Just as good communication and respect are essential aspects needed for intimacy in marriage, these are vital if we want to truly know God's heart and will.

Jesus gives us the power to overcome demonic oppression. We cannot receive this power without first having constant and consistent fellowship with Him. We fellowship with Jesus by reading His Word and praying. Fellowship produces faith. Faith produces and releases power. Power puts the enemy to flight.

We are to wait upon the Lord. This means we are to be willing to wait for God's answers and direction no matter how long it takes. In 1 Samuel 13:7-14, we have the example of Saul not waiting for Samuel as instructed by the Lord. Because Saul did not obey and wait as instructed by God, he lost his kingdom.

We must learn to minister to the Lord. Ministering to the Lord means that we praise Him, exalt Him and thank Him for all He has done and is doing. We should develop fellowship with Jesus in which we are giving our heart, soul, and time to Him. When we give to Jesus, He promises that He will empower us.

Pride Assignment

Identify prideful attitudes in your heart. Review the list of prideful attitudes given in this chapter.

List those areas in which you sin toward others.

Identify and write about how your prideful attitudes have made you behave in an ungodly manner.

Identify rebellious attitudes in your heart. Then, write down how your rebellion has affected your relationship with God and those you love.

What negative consequences have you suffered because of pride and rebellion? What changes are you going to make to defeat your sinful attitudes and behaviors?

Identify areas of shame in your heart because of your sin. Make amends to others when offenses have taken place. Ask God's forgiveness for each specific offense and sinful attitude.

After you've written out your answers to the above questions, ask relatives or friends to answer the same questions concerning you. Then, examine and ponder the difference in the answers. What is God revealing to you?

Saul Attitudes

God is continuously calling us into accountability for the type of attitudes we have toward those in our home and those we associate with on a daily basis. Many times, our attitudes and responses to others are rooted in sin. When we fail to recognize our sinful attitudes, we wound others and bring bondage upon ourselves and those we love. Saul is an excellent example of an individual who failed to deal with his sin and was eventually destroyed. David is an example of an individual who sinned, but whose heart was one of repentance. David was willing to allow God to bring him into brokenness to make him whole and acceptable to God.

There are serious problems in a marriage when any of the attitudes and responses to a spouse have been based upon the characteristics exhibited in Saul's life. When we have a humble spirit before the Lord, repentance in our heart, and a willingness to accept pain, rejection, and discipline from the Lord, we are being made and molded in Christ's image.

Characteristics of Saul

God called Saul to be king of Israel. The following are some of Saul's characteristics:

- Impressive, unequal among the Israelites
- Attractive
- Sought God for direction
- An anointed leader
- Filled with the Spirit of God and prophesied
- Close to God - God told Saul to "do whatever your hand finds to do I am with you" (1 Samuel 10:7).
- Had a changeable heart

Saul certainly had all the qualities, characteristics and promises from God to become very successful and to be blessed by the Lord. What happened to him that he fell out of grace? Let's look at what Saul allowed to enter into his heart that resulted in his fall and destruction.

- Saul did not keep God's command to obey Him. He was not after God's heart. The battles became a personal victory rather than God's victory.
- Saul cursed (bound) his people by his demands. The people became desperate and committed sin by eating meat with blood in it.
- Saul responded irrationally out of his desire for victory. The priest rather than Saul says, "Let's ask God what to do." This introduces a power-play.
- Saul was willing to put his son to death to have victory even though Jonathan heard God and delivered the Israelites from the Philistines. He had no compassion for his family.
- Saul was told by God to destroy all the Amalekites and everything they owned. He disobeyed and turned away from God's Word. Materialism and possessions were too important to him as they signified power.
- Saul set up a monument in his own honor.
- He did not listen to God.
- He allowed rebellion in his heart, which led to contacting a medium (witchcraft).
- He blamed others for his actions. He refused to look at his own sinful heart.
- Saul justified his behavior. He had an attitude of denial.
- Saul was deceptive. He made promises and did not keep them.
- His anger and jealousy led to murderous thoughts in his heart, which resulted in his attempting to kill David and his son, Jonathan.
- God sent an evil spirit to torment him.
- Saul was frequently dismayed and terrorized. He could only be comforted by someone that had the Spirit of God dwelling in him (David).
- His kingdom was snatched from his hands by God and given to David.
- Saul committed suicide.

Characteristics of David

- He had a fine appearance and handsome features.
- He spoke well.
- David was a brave man and a warrior.
- The Lord was with him.

- He was a man of faith – God will deliver.
- David claimed victory in the name of the Lord, not by the sword.
- David was humble, and God made him successful.
- David believed God's Word and applied it to his life.
- He had a repentant heart.
- He obeyed God.

The attitudes in David's heart were as follows:

- He would not touch God's anointed no matter what Saul said or did to him.
- He would not lift his hand against those who humiliated or disgraced him.
- He knew he had done no wrong.
- David had no rebellion in his heart.
- He believed that the Lord would avenge the wrong done to him.
- He believed God would vindicate and deliver him.
- His heart believed that God would consider his cause.
- David would not hurt his enemy, Saul.
- David repented when he had wrong attitudes in his heart, which resulted in him changing his behavior or plans.
- He lived a life of humility.
- David was willing to be broken before God and others. He would state, "Maybe God is done with me." His attitude was that God's plans and ways were best. He submitted to God's plans.
- David found his strength in the Lord, His God.
- David's brokenness before God made him the apple of God's eye and a king after God's own heart.
- David sought wisdom from godly individuals.

David had a covenant relationship with God. We have a covenant relationship with God, and we have a covenant relationship in marriage. What kind of attitudes do we exhibit to our spouses? A Saul attitude or a David attitude?

Saul Attitudes in Marriage

- I don't care what you think, I am going to do it my way.
- My needs are more important than yours.
- If you don't meet my needs, I will not be there for you.

- If you are going to treat me that way, I'll_________________.
- I'm the boss of this home.
- You are insensitive and make stupid decisions.
- No matter how hard I try nothing changes.
- I need to fend for myself, you sure won't meet my needs.
- I don't care what you think, I'm going to ____________.
- God has put me as the head of this home. Therefore, you and our family must do as I say.
- I'm justified in my responses because you hurt me.
- If you don't meet my needs, I will get them met somewhere else.
- I'll meet my desires at all costs.
- This is not my problem. It is your problem.

Saul Attitudes Assignment

List the Saul-like responses you have had toward your spouse.

What kind of responses should you have toward your spouse if you have a "David's heart"?

How are you going to change your Saul attitudes and responses?

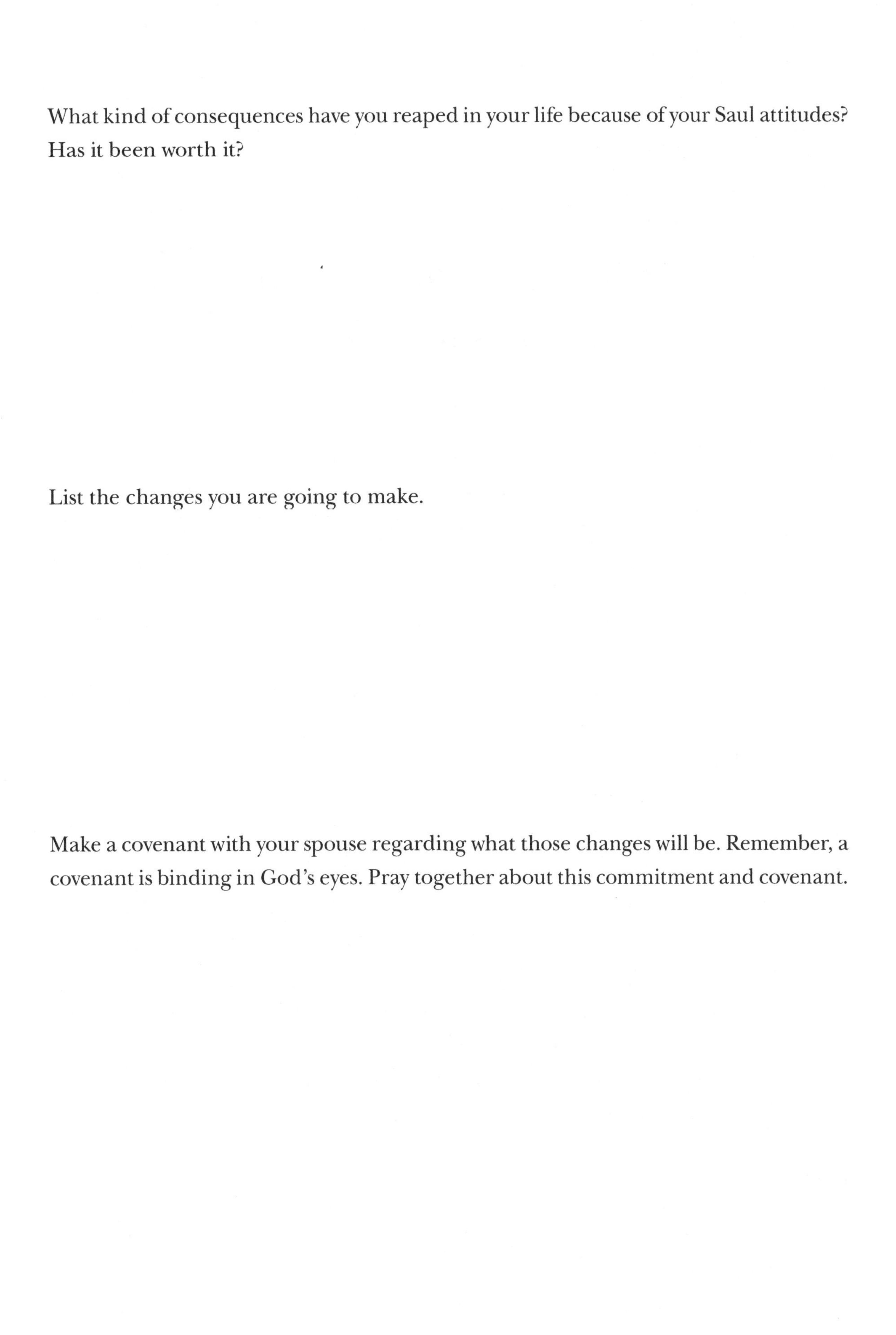

What kind of consequences have you reaped in your life because of your Saul attitudes? Has it been worth it?

List the changes you are going to make.

Make a covenant with your spouse regarding what those changes will be. Remember, a covenant is binding in God's eyes. Pray together about this commitment and covenant.

How the Enemy Works

Satan works to tempt us by attacking our mind. The option facing us is to accept his lies and thoughts, or reject them and choose to stand on the truth of God's Word. If we listen to Satan, he will take us down the following path of destruction:

Rejects Truth	Accepts and Chooses Lies
Mind	Chooses the carnal nature—accepts a lying thought rather than rejecting it.
Mind	The enemy makes suggestions or situations appear pleasing and rewarding.
Mind and Body	Embraces the sin. Physically and emotionally we respond. Behaviors exhibit our sinful responses.
Oppression	The mind becomes more controlled by the sin. It does not submit to God's laws and the Word. This leads to disobedience.
Heart Hardens	Demons attack our mind to oppress our thinking. Our heart becomes hard and we become rebellious. Truth is rejected and lies are believed.
Bondage	The oppression increases in other areas of our life. We are deceived by sin, and bondage increases. Demons enter.
Seared Conscience	If unsaved, demons can possess us. If saved, demons have us bound, and our life is havoc.

Break the Cycle

1. Submit to God. If we submit, the devil has no legal right to stay. He has to flee (James 4:7).

2. Take personal responsibility for our sinful thoughts and behavior. The victory is ours. If we continue to allow the enemy to control our mind and heart, we have given him a legal foothold in our life, and he brings death.
3. Repent of sin, which means to turn away and "forsake." We do not go back (Luke 13:5; Matt. 4:7).
4. Break strongholds and demonic oppression.
5. Attack the enemy with the "Written Word" (Matt. 4:4-10). Satan has to leave.

Prayer

Dear Jesus. I ask You to forgive me for allowing the stronghold of ____ [name it] *to operate in my life. I command the power of this stronghold to be broken over my family and me. I ask, Jesus, that You forgive all the members of my family, going back through all my past generations, of any sins they have committed that allowed this stronghold into our family line. Jesus, by the authority of Your Word, I come against this stronghold of* ______________________________ [name it] *and command it broken off of me. I pull down any ungodly mindset or structures that it has built in my mind and heart. I choose this day to walk in righteousness. Jesus, where this stronghold has controlled me, I ask that You replace it with Your love, Word, and character. Cleanse me from all my sins in the area where I have allowed* ______________________________ [name it], *and set me free. Thank You, Jesus, for forgiving my sins and breaking the power of this stronghold.*

How the Enemy Works Assignment

List the ways Satan entices you by your flesh.

Describe the way Satan entices you by the lust of the eyes.

Describe the way Satan entices you by the boastful pride of life.

What sinful thoughts do you struggle with?

List the steps you need to take to overcome your sinful thoughts and behavior.

Memorize scriptures that will help you overcome when Satan tempts you. Quote these scriptures daily until you have won the battle.

Prayer

> *Dear Jesus, I ask You to forgive me for having pride in my heart. I acknowledge that I have thought more highly of myself than I have of others. Many times, Jesus, I have wanted or demanded my own way. Jesus, forgive me and help me to have a humble and contrite spirit before You and others. Give me a servant's heart. Take all my sin that is in my heart and destroy the roots of rebellion and wickedness. I desire to live my life in obedience to You and Your Word. Lord, help me to seek Your wisdom and knowledge. In those areas where I have sinned by not following Your ways, I ask Your forgiveness. Cleanse me from that sin and set me free. Thank You, Jesus, for forgiving my sins and helping me to become more Christ-like. In Jesus' Name, Amen.*

Note the drawing on the next page. Do you see how sinful thoughts and behaviors prevent you from receiving all the blessings that God wants to place in your heart and life?

TEMPTATION

Chooses to accept idea or words of darkness.

Carnal nature chooses to obey.

Enemy makes suggestions/ situations appear pleasing & rewarding.

Embrace sin.

Body exhibits sinful behavior.

Mind more controlled by sin/choosing not to submit to God's law.

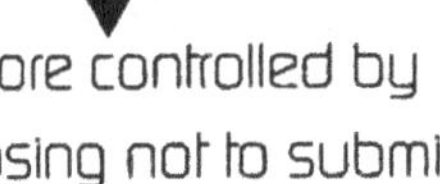

Demons free to attack mind & oppress thinking/become hard-hearted, stubborn, rebellious, reject truth, lies manifested.

Oppression Increases. Sin deceives you. Demons enter.

Difficulty receiving and hearing word of God/ reject God's ways.

Seared Conscience/ conviction gone.

Reject words of light.

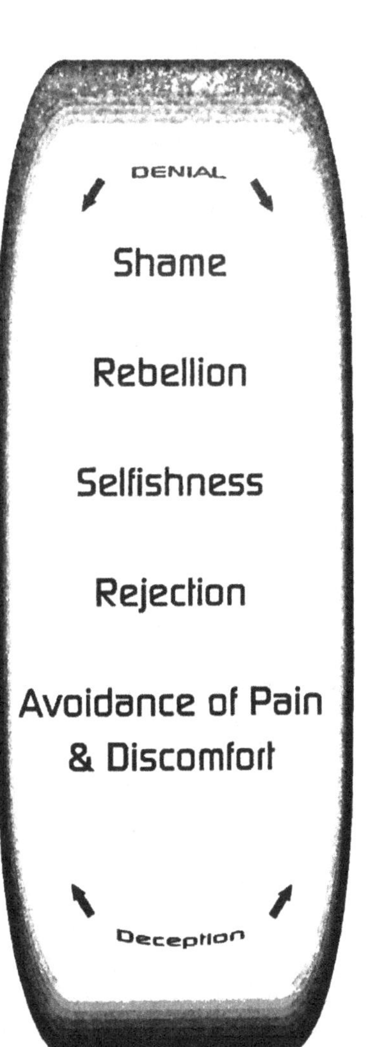

Destruction to Victory—Testimony

The following testimony is written by a couple who desire to share with others how God is able to heal the deepest wounds and restore a marriage that was on the brink of death.

Husband's Testimony

As a child, I was physically and mentally abused, and ultimately abandoned by my parents. Because of that, I had very low self-esteem and was very angry at God and at life. I first attempted suicide at age sixteen. I did not know how to show or receive affection, and I felt so alone. I was a mixed up and lonely kid who decided to join the military. I went into the military with a lot of emotional problems and came out of it after the war with Post Traumatic Stress Disorder. Because of the abuse I experienced during my childhood and the trauma experienced in the military, I was now dealing with deep rooted resentment and anger. I medicated myself with alcohol and drugs. As a result, I was in and out of mental health and rehabilitation programs for years. I eventually got married and that marriage ended in divorce. I lost everything, and my ex-wife eventually died from drug abuse. If this is how my life was going to be, I prayed to God to end my suffering by taking my life. I was slowly killing myself with alcohol and drugs.

There is one thing I did well and that was work. I am a workaholic. I have been blessed with an artistic eye, which made me excel in the hair styling industry. When I was working in a salon, I met my present wife. She asked me if I wanted to go to church with her. At first I told her that she didn't want to mess with a guy like me because I am bad news. I eventually went to church and came to know Jesus as my Lord and Savior. I was born again, but I still had a lot of problems. I was still suffering from PTSD and medicating myself by drinking and drugging. Oftentimes, I did not come home at night to my wife.

When my first son was born, I was afraid that I wouldn't be a good father. During this time, my drinking and drugging got worse. Then son number two came. I had such low self-esteem, I was sure I was going to mess this up like everything else in my life. My wife and I went through marriage counseling after marriage counseling. Even our pastor friend who was counseling us was about to throw in the towel. We went to a pre-marriage fellowship at our church and met a couple who told us about Sydney. We went to Sydney a few times, but we were still on shaky ground. She called us one day and asked if we wanted to go to this program she had for married couples. The first time we attended it was hard as I was still dealing with my life the way I always did.

One day God spoke to me in a way that really opened my eyes and made me realize He was always there no matter what. He reminded me that He had given me a home with a beautiful wife, kids, and my own business. Even though the devil kept me blinded with self-doubt and self-pity, I now wanted to live and keep my marriage. Sydney's teaching gave us a new way of looking at our marriage and how we have bitter-root judgments and bitter-root expectancies that the devil uses against us. Working with other couples made us realize that we are not alone in this battle. The workbook has given us new weapons to fight the devil who comes to steal, kill and destroy. As a couple, we are still working on getting our hearts healed, but it is good to know that God is with us every step of the way. The Breaking Free program has changed me as a person. Everyday God is at the center of my life. I now have a new beginning with God. I recognize the importance of praying with my wife, and we read the Bible together daily. God has shown me that life is worth living. I now know I have a purpose in life. I am also able to understand how the woundedness from my childhood has influenced my thoughts, behaviors and belief system. I am not as anxious as I used to be, and I have surrounded myself with men and women who support and pray for and with me. God is not finished with me yet. Every day as I grow, I am thankful. I know that God has more instore for me, and that He is always with me wherever I go. I just have to be honest with myself, pray, read the Word, and share with others how I feel so God can continue His work within me. I am blessed. Philippians 4:13 says, "I have strength for all things in Christ who empowers me [I am ready for anything and equal to anything through Him who infuses inner strength into me; I am self-sufficient in Christ's sufficiency]" (AMPC).

Wife's Testimony

The Breaking Free Program has changed my life, my marriage, my relationship with my children, and relationships with others as well. It has taught me to first confess the scars and wounds of my past to Jesus and bring them to light and have others pray for me. Matthew 18:20 says, "When two of you get together on anything at all on earth and make a prayer of it, my Father in heaven goes into action" (MSG). Anger, control, and fear have gripped my life because of my upbringing. I am an only child and was always told what to do. I could never make decisions on my own. I felt as if I could never do anything right and was never accepted and loved for who I am. This made me become bitter. Being the perfectionist I am, I tried to do everything right without making mistakes. I had self-doubt because I did what was expected.

As I began to journal about the hurt from my mom, I recognized who I had become because of my bitter-root judgments and my bitter-root expectancies. Through prayer and deliverance there has been a release in my spirit. Because I have forgiven my mom, I have healing in my heart and our relationship has gotten better. Although my parents may never change or they may still react the same way, I no longer have those feelings of anger and guilt toward them.

I have realized that I brought my wounded issues into my marriage as well. When we started this program, my husband and I were on the verge of divorce. It was very painful for me to deal with my husband's PTSD, alcoholism, and drug addiction. Being hurt over and over again made me not trust him. Since I struggle with control and trust issues, I sometimes still have a hard time dealing with this, but seeing changes within my husband keeps me growing stronger day by day.

The only way I was able to see beyond everything else was to first work on me. That was very hard to do. Looking back and remembering how I felt as a child was not easy, and it brought up a lot of bad memories. Now, because I have examined and confessed my offenses, bitter-root judgments, and bitter-root expectancies to Jesus and the Breaking Free group, I have the faith to see things through God's eyes. It's not about what my natural eyes can see, it's about what God's Word says. It may not be how my perfectionist mind would like to see it, but everything happens in God's perfect timing and way.

Rain or shine, my husband and I made the commitment to stick with the program. We eventually decided to attend the program a second time. There have been many positive changes along the way. I may not be able to fix or change my husband, but through journaling, praying and confessing my past and sin to God and others, I have accepted my husband for who he is. I also have a better understanding of myself and where I stand in each season of our life.

By working on me and my woundedness, I am able to take a step back and view everything in my life from a new and different perspective. The things that used to bother me are not the main issues anymore. I am able to let go and move on with no anger. I know that God has cleansed my heart inside and out. There have been times I didn't feel like doing what I needed to do, but I kept on doing what I knew to do whether it was praying, sharing, encouraging others, or attending the program. If we keep on doing what we know to do, God honors that and in turn He will bless us one hundred fold.

The second time around with the Breaking Free Program, we were blessed to renew our wedding vows. Now, my husband and I have become closer. We read the Bible and pray together every day. What I love the most is when we sit or lay together and share our hearts with one another. Every little step counts. I used to look for big changes to happen in my own life and in my marriage. But when I take a look at the past ten years with my husband, every little step along the way took us to where we are today. Making a change requires doing whatever it takes even though we can't see the outcome.

Romans 5:4-5 says, "There's more to come: we continue to shout our praise even when we're hemmed in with troubles, because we know how troubles can develop passionate patience in us and how that patience in turn forges the tempered steel of virtue, keeping us alert for whatever God will do next" (MSG).

There will never be a perfect road, but now I have the comfort in knowing my husband and I are able to communicate and understand each other at a different and deeper level than we used to. We are reaping the fruit of our commitment to God and each other. Everyone has a different testimony to share, and each one is unique. Healing and recovery are available to everyone if we choose to look at the things that hurt the most. By being honest and open about our past woundedness, God can heal the things that are rooted up on the inside of us. We just have to be transparent, willing to talk about our woundedness with others, and allow God to do the rest. If we allow God to do the work needed in us, our life will never be the same. I walk in God's blessings and restoration. Thank You, Jesus.

Traits of a Healthy Family

Healthy Relationships

Feelings are nurtured and shared. You affirm and support one another and admit your mistakes. Trust is nurtured by doing what you say and following through with your commitments. It is okay to have conflict and realize that your spouse will not meet all yours needs because God will. It is okay to feel.

Healthy Communication Patterns

Listen to and hear each other's feelings, ideas and beliefs. Do not speak to one another in a sarcastic, demanding or demeaning way. Respond in a loving way. Listening to one another results in your heart being open to each other and developing intimacy. Respect your partner. No self-righteous statements. Do not build your case. Do not push his/her buttons or take inventory of his/her behavior or responses. Respect yourself and take responsibility for your actions and the consequences of things done in your past. If you take the victim role, you are experiencing anger and need to deal with it. What you and your spouse share needs to be kept confidential. Rid yourself of expectations. As someone said, "Expectations are premeditated resentments."

Healthy Spiritual Life

Parents are to stand firm and believe what the Word of God says. Fathers are to be the spiritual leader of the home, helping children work out their faith, praying for them daily and teaching them to pray. Parents are to pray together and walk in obedience to the teachings of Christ. Lay hands on your children and put the armor of God on them every day.

Healthy Balance of Work and Play

Have the gift of laughter and humor in your home. Play games together. Humor is never to be sarcastic, embarrassing or cutting. Leave your work at the office, but do take the children to work so they learn balance of play and work. Teach children the principle of giving. Teach them to revere hard work and purpose. Believe that you have the ability to effectively and successfully parent your children. God has equipped you for every good work.

Bless Your Family

Speak words of affirmation to your family. Affectionately touch them and tell them how valuable and worthwhile they are. Tell them frequently that you love them. Hug them often and tell them what an awesome person they are. Do not compare them to others or reward them according to their performance. Know your child's love language.

Seven Principles for a Biblical Family

Fight for Your Family

> "For you were once darkness, but now you are light in the Lord. Walk as children of light ... finding out what is acceptable to the Lord." (Eph. 5:8, 10 NKJV)

War against anything that would try to destroy your family. Spiritual warfare and prayer are essential. Pray daily for your family, erecting spiritual boundaries the enemy of your soul is forbidden to cross. Don't ignore spiritual warfare or you will experience the destruction the enemy can bring into your family.

Affirm Each Other Continually

> "Do not let any unwholesome talk come out of your mouths, but only what is helpful for building others up according to their needs, that it may benefit those who listen." (Eph. 4:29 NIV)

Speak words of affirmation to each other daily. Have a servant's heart. That is, be more interested in uplifting others than you being uplifted. See each other as a team with a heart of submission one to another. You are equal in Christ.

Make Good Communication a Priority

> "Pleasant words are like a honeycomb, sweetness to the soul and health to the bones." (Prov. 16:24 NKJV)

Share your feelings with each other. Be willing to listen to your family members without judging them. Accept them whether you agree with them or not. Honor their opinions.

Have honesty without anger. Apologize each time you say something that offends or hurts another. Continue to break dysfunctional cycles from your past that hurt your present relationships.

Install Reverence for God

> "You shall love the Lord your God with all your heart, with all your soul, and with all your strength. And, these words which I command you today shall be in your heart. You shall teach them diligently to your children, and shall talk of them when you sit in your house, when you walk by the way, when you lie down and when you rise up." (Deut. 6:5-7 NKJV)

Teach your children that reverence and obedience to God will result in God's purpose for their life being fulfilled and will bring abundant blessings. Instruct and teach them to fear the Lord. This means that they are to understand the holiness and supremacy of God and honor Him.

Love Each Other Unconditionally

> "Walk in love, as Christ also has loved us and given himself for us, an offering and a sacrifice to God for a sweet-smelling aroma." (Eph. 5:2 NKJV)

Tell your children that you love them. Tell your children you are sorry when you wound them and ask their forgiveness. In your mind, separate their behavior from who they are as a person. You are to hate the sin, but love the sinner.

Teach Your Children Responsibility

Teach and train your children that they are responsible for their actions, behaviors and attitudes. They need to learn that there are consequences to sin. They also need to learn that trust worthiness and responsibility reaps benefits such as respect from others, integrity and honor.

Teach Your Children How To Understand and React Positively to Failure

The character of an individual is clearly shown when he or she understands that failing does not mean he or she is a failure as a person. Failure is something that happens on the road to success. Teach your children that failure builds their character if they see it from a Christian perspective.

Symptoms of a Dysfunctional Family

- We guess at what normal is.
- We have difficulty following projects through from beginning to end.
- We lie when it would be just as easy to tell the truth.
- We judge ourselves without mercy.
- We have difficulty having fun, or all we want to do is to play.
- We take ourselves too seriously.
- We have difficulty with intimate relationships.
- We overreact to changes, even those over which we have no control.
- We feel different from other people.
- Many tasks that ought to be easy we find difficult to accomplish.
- We constantly seek approval and affirmation, but expect disapproval and rejection.
- We are either super-responsible or super-irresponsible.
- We are extremely loyal, even in the face of evidence that loyalty is not deserved.
- We look for immediate gratification, instead of deferred gratification.
- We lock ourselves into a course of action instead of considering other options or the consequences of our actions.
- We unconsciously seek tension and crisis and then complain about the results.
- We fear rejection or abandonment, yet reject or abandon others.
- We fear failure but habitually sabotage success.
- We sometimes refuse to try, though we know our efforts would benefit us or those we love.
- We fear criticism and judgment, yet criticize others and judge them for not meeting our needs.

- We manage our time poorly and don't set priorities that work well for us and those we love.
- We do not listen to others; we are often into our own little world.

As a result of the dysfunction (trauma or unmet needs from our parents), we have a warped image of who we are. When those needs are not met, we display fear and anger. Then, we buy into the lies about who we think we are and believe "We are what we do." We feel attacked, threatened and unsafe, so we choose not to feel, talk about our feelings or trust. Rejection enters our heart, and we act on the lies we believe. We deny we have a problem and refuse to work on root causes. Rather than accept responsibility for our behavior, we blame others for how we are or what is happening to us. The blame is rooted in our feelings of shame, rejection, rage and fear.

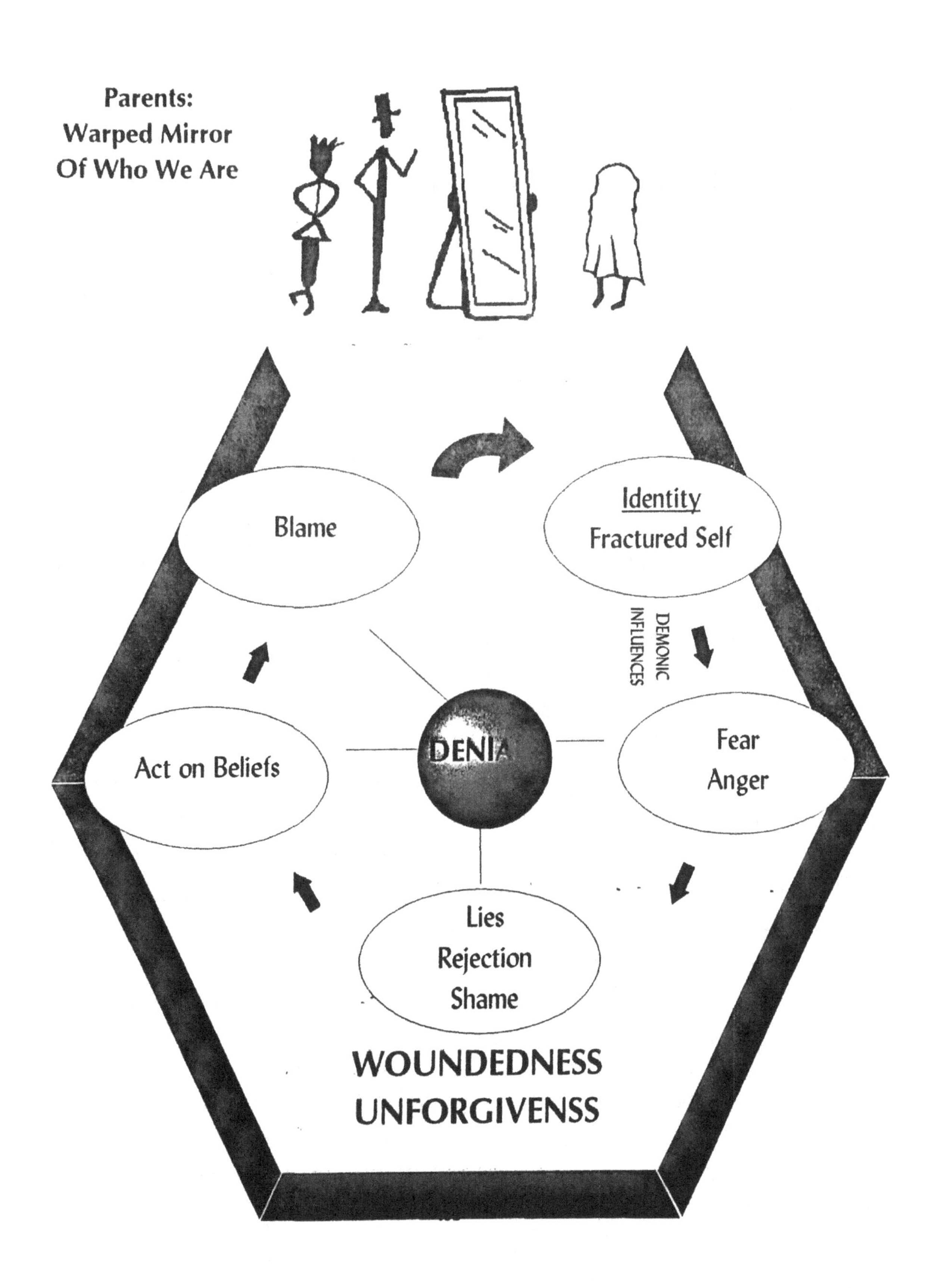
Parents:
Warped Mirror
Of Who We Are
Blame
Identity
Fractured Self
DEMONIC
INFLUENCES
DENIA
Act on Beliefs
Fear
Anger
Lies
Rejection
Shame
WOUNDEDNESS
UNFORGIVENSS

Delivered from Addiction—Testimony

The following is a testimony from woman who was delivered from addiction.

As a little girl, I was molested by my maternal step-grandfather. It took place for a week or two every summer. It began when I was four or five years old and lasted until my parents caught him when I was twelve years old. He raped me when I was ten years old. That is when he told me, "I only love you like this." Sickening as it sounds, I came to the conclusion that sex was "true love." I even started to believe that my dad and my other grandpa didn't love me because they did not love me the same way my step-grandfather did.

When I was twelve, my paternal grandparents gave me a horse. I was favored by them and they were very special to me. I enjoyed my horse for quite a while, and then he became ill. My parents had to get rid of the horse, and I felt as though I had lost my life. In a sense, I did. That is when I started searching for love to fill the void caused by that painful loss.

The first thing I tried to fill the void with was alcohol. Alcohol only helped for a while. Then, I became quite promiscuous. I was looking for a male to give me the kind of love my grandfather had given me. Combined with the alcohol, that only gave me a reputation as an easy girl. I was rapidly confirming that rumor by my behavior. In the process, I was turned on to marijuana. I started with just a gram every week or two, and easily worked my way up to an eighth (3-4 grams) every two or three days. The alcohol and drugs became a prerequisite for "life." They enabled me to cope. I soon learned that I liked cocaine better than all the drugs I tried. I snorted it until someone gave me a spoon hit. That's a way to smoke it. That high was what I thought I was looking for. I just kept smoking more and more, hoping for that same rush again. I spent every penny I could get my sticky little fingers on to buy drugs.

My parents and siblings had a difficult time being around me because of my drug use. I stole money and lied to my parents all the time. They finally chose to apply the tough love principle and made me move out of their home. I was angry and hateful to them for not accepting my lifestyle. As I look back upon that time, I know their tough love was what I needed. Once out of my parents' home, I moved from one house to another, still trying to fill that hunger in my life. Men didn't do it. Drugs and alcohol didn't either. I figured it must be this part of the United States, and I just wanted to get away. I saw no options. My parents wanted me to go to counseling. I chose a counselor out of town. I figured I would be able to get a break from my present circumstances. When I was in counseling, the counselor told me things I didn't want to hear.

I decided to go to California without telling anyone where I was going. The time spent in California was a big mistake. However, I didn't see it that way until a year later, and I wouldn't admit that to anyone. The drugs in California were everywhere. I thought I would go down there and start a new life. I was extremely immature and foolish. After having a relationship with a very abusive boyfriend, who was a gang member and sold drugs, I finally came back home.

After I returned from California, I continued in the same behavior. I was on a party binge when I drove my car off the freeway into a tree. I was seriously hurt. The bones on the left side of my face were all crushed.

That was it for me, no more partying. At least until one night when I met a man who got me back into drinking. During this relationship, I moved to Seattle. Off to the big city. Same story, different town. After getting fired from every job I tried to hold down, I saw an ad in the paper. It read, "$100.00 a day, waitress needed." Yes! This must be the dream job. Well, okay it was at a strip joint. No biggy, I won't take off my clothes. When I found out the money strippers were making, I was blown away. They were making $300-$600 a day. I told myself I was only going to do it for two weeks so I could get my longstanding debts paid off. My two weeks turned into four years. After about one year of dancing, I found out about a club that was much classier. Don't get me wrong, sin is sin. I just didn't care about sin then. It was all about looks and the money I could get for my drugs. In the process of my dancing, I hooked up with well-known drug dealers in town. That of course only fed into my drug problem. It is only by the grace of our MIGHTY GOD that I am still alive to talk about HIS POWER.

At the tail-end of my dancing days, I was smoking about $300-$500 of crack a day. That was about how much money I was making per day. I had heard how good the money was down in Florida--$1,000 a day on a regular basis. I thought I was pregnant and knew that kind of money could get me an abortion and other things I wanted. I made plans to meet some of my friends down there, and I was on my way.

God had other plans. I met someone down there who had all the material things that I always wanted. He was clean and sober, so I stayed clean too. For the first time in years, I was off all substances for ten days. I was on cloud nine. I came home and went over to a friend's house with the real desire to stay clean. I couldn't. I was starting to come to terms with the fact that I had a severe drug problem, and I knew I was pregnant. I knew that I could not have this child. It would not be fair to bring a baby into the world with all the drugs I had given it. This was my fifth pregnancy. I'd had a miscarriage a year before and three other abortions. A few years later when I came back to God, God healed me from the pain and self-hatred I had over aborting those babies. The Lord gave me mental pictures of each of my babies, and I named each child.

I just couldn't go through another abortion because I wanted to get my life back on track with God. You see, I was raised in a loving, Christian home and had accepted Jesus into my heart when I was six years old. I knew God and always believed that someday I would come back to Him. It was the molestation, painful loss of my horse, and wrong choices that took me down the wrong track. I did go clean and pleaded with God that if He gave me a healthy baby, I would never go back to my old lifestyle again. It was very hard, but God knew my heart and heard my cry. He gave me a beautiful, healthy son. He is now five years old. He is strong, healthy, smart, and very handsome. He is a blessing from God! He should have been born an addict, but God did a miracle. I call him "my miracle baby." That he surely is!

Walking out of addiction is a very difficult task. I personally could not have succeeded without God at my side and without the prayers of my parents and others. Many times God simply carried me.

During my drug years, there had been many warrants out for my arrest because of unpaid driving tickets. In the last five years, I have cleaned up all my warrants. My driving record is now clean. I've gone back to college and have only five quarters left to have my degree as a licensed alcohol and substance abuse counselor. Before I give you the final punch line, my high school GPA was below 1.0 my junior and senior year. Okay ... get this, I got a scholarship at my college and have maintained a 3.3 or better for the last year. I'm pretty jazzed! Praise Jesus!

God has delivered me from all the drugs and sexual sin in my life. He has also freed me from a lot of spiritual bondage that I had opened myself up to over the years. I now know what it is to walk in freedom. I will never say that going clean is easy, it isn't. I will always say it's worth it! God has blessed me beyond my wildest imagination. I say, "LET GO, AND LET GOD!"

Characteristics of an Addictive Personality

The following are characteristics of an addictive personality:

- You are selfish—your needs are the most important.
- You have an inner emptiness that you are constantly trying to fill.
- Your life seems to have little meaning or purpose.
- You are always needing extra affirmations in order to feel that you are acceptable and worthwhile.
- You are very hard on yourself and actually hate yourself.
- You have excessive guilt and shame.
- You are angry.
- You repress your feelings and emotionally withdraw from those close to you.
- You occasionally have emotional numbness.
- You have inner tension—you cannot rest.
- You are afraid to risk.
- You struggle with fear of failure or rejection.
- You have hidden dependency on others—if they meet your needs then all is well with you and life.
- You feel your needs are unmet.
- You have trouble with authority figures.
- You are rebellious.
- You blame others for your problems rather than take responsibility for your own behavior.
- You have poor coping skills.
- You are a wishful thinker or dreamer.
- You have never emotionally grown up.

- You do not set healthy boundaries for yourself.
- You are impulsive and/or compulsive.
- You cannot parent yourself.
- You rely on others when difficulties arise and are angry when they do not meet your expectations.
- You have intimacy problems. It is hard for you to give or receive quality love.
- You cannot enjoy life nor have fun. Everything is work.
- You close your heart down to others, and they complain that you emotionally shut them out.
- Your communication is rigid.

ADDICTION

Today we live in a society that is multi-addicted. Addiction plays a major role in the breakup of many marriages and families. Individual lives are destroyed or nearly destroyed emotionally, physically, financially, and spiritually because of addictive behaviors and addictive thinking patterns. There are many different addictions and all of them bring bondage to a person's life. A person may suffer from a substance addiction, behavioral addiction or both.

The following are examples of various addictions:

Approval	Alcohol
Relationships	Drugs
Television	Food
Exercise	Sex
Adrenaline	Work
Computer (toys)	

What makes a person an addict? Many circumstances are contributive factors to addiction. However, one common element in every addict's life is neediness. Most addicts don't even recognize that they have a lot of unmet needs and pain in their heart. Addicts often learn at a young age to avoid the real issues in their heart. Because of painful circumstances in their life, which usually occur during childhood, they have learned to turn off their feelings. Consequently, they have not dealt with unresolved childhood pain. Many addicts make the statement that they become addicted because of peer pressure. On occasion this may be true. But for most individuals, when they allow the Holy Spirit to show them what happened to their heart as a child, they are able to discover that hurtful memories, events, or feelings they suppressed and never dealt with were the actual causes.

As individuals suppress, more often repress, they are not identifying the real issues in their heart that led them into addictive thinking. One of the first stages of addiction is to blame others for their problems. Blame causes us to avoid the real issues in our heart. It is always the "other guy's" fault when life doesn't go well. When addicts blame another for their problems, they are not being honest about the pain of the inner child and how that pain is fueling behaviors and beliefs that create an addict's out-of-control lifestyle. Satan now has a secret weapon he can use against them. That weapon is DENIAL. God cannot heal when we do not honestly deal with our sinful attitudes and responses.

Denial is like a huge roadblock that prevents us from seeing truth and walking into freedom. The mind becomes conditioned not to look at the needs of the inner child. *To look* means to take responsibility for how we have behaved or responded to others, both as a child and as an adult. Oftentimes, it seems as though we would incur less feelings of pain if we ignore the wounded child inside. This mentality is a work of deception by Satan, the enemy of our souls. Satan does not want anyone to look at truth. The truth is that looking at one's pain and getting healed takes a relatively short period of time. That time period is nothing compared to living with pain for the rest of our life and reaping the consequences of our behavior.

God tells us to bring our sinful thoughts and actions to Him so that He can heal us. When we refuse to do so, we are being disobedient and rebellious to God. The pain remains in our heart, and we're kept in bondage. Hell has a foothold in our heart, mind and emotions. One becomes a slave to one's area of bondage. Freedom comes from honest evaluation of one's self and submitting to God. Then, the addictive cycle can be broken.

It is important to realize that stopping the addictive *behavior* does not mean that we have walked out of our addiction. An alcoholic or drug addict may no longer be abusing alcohol or drugs, but they still think and behave like an addict, even after ten years of sobriety! Many individuals who have been delivered by the Lord from drugs or alcohol consider themselves free from addiction. But people are not free from addiction until they have dealt with their addictive thinking. That means looking at and understanding how their belief system operates in them. Most addicts would state that they know what they believe, but when required to examine what they believe, they may be surprised to find that what they believe *in their head* is different than what they believe *in their heart*. Our actions and how we respond to others and to life come out of our heart.

God says our heart is what is deceptively wicked. He does not say it is our mind that is wicked. The Lord tells us we must renew our mind and get our heart healed. People must look at their woundedness and the judgments, vows, and lies they believe to come into complete healing. Then, there must be prayer for healing in all these areas

Addicts have a deeply warped self-concept. The paradox of tremendous pride and abject self-worthlessness can inhabit an individual. With these individuals, it is either black or white. They are either beyond challenge, intellectually superior to others, or worthy of everything bad that can be said about them. There seems to be no in-between. Addicts are never okay just by "being." They can't understand how they can be loved and accepted for who they are without performance or without comparison to others. Their pride, and maybe even some of the driven perfectionism, is just a cover-up for deep-rooted self-hatred, shame and worthlessness. The following are statements addicts believe:

- If I believe others are inferior to me, then I can feel good about myself.
- If I can just maintain an appearance of perfection, others will admire, need and trust in me.
- When others think highly of me, I will be able to think highly of myself.
- Any need of or reliance on me, indicates others are inferior and I am better. I would rather feel that way than to feel inferior, wrong or imperfect in comparison to others because that would make me unworthy of love and approval.

In short, these individuals are addicted to others' approval. Without it they crash into a crumpled pile of self-pity and worthlessness. At the center of it all is a tremendous preoccupation with self and how the "I" stands in relation to others. It is all about them.

Some addicts never arrive at the defense of pride and perfectionism. They remain in the "defeated" posture—never expecting to feel better than anyone else. They always feel awful and have very low self-esteem. That pain is so great that it will ultimately lead them to "use" again. The drug numbs their pain and for a short period of time they feel better.

A prideful addict can become an abased addict within moments. When denial cracks and floods of realization come in, arrogant and self-assured egos can collapse into blubbering confessions of "How awful I am!" This can be the "bottom" which addicts must sometimes hit to begin turning their life around. Other times, it is just a temporary breech in their defenses or a manipulative attempt to get others off their back for a while. Sometimes they may not be fully aware of their manipulation. Once recovered, they'll retreat into the same mindset, reinforced by a more painful than usual episode of conscious worthlessness. It's a lonely, terrible, painful, double life.

For addicts to come into total healing, they must examine their belief system and look at what they have opened themselves up to spiritually. Since drugs and alcohol consumption open a person spiritually to a spirit of witchcraft, there needs to be prayer for deliverance (Deut. 18:9-15; Gal. 5:20).

The root word for witchcraft is the word *pharmakeia*, which means drugs or pharmacy. Therefore, scripture teaches that when people take drugs (alcohol is a drug) for sinful pleasure, they are opening themselves up to witchcraft. Whoever opens themselves to witchcraft is also entering into rebellion. 1 Samuel 15:23 says, "For rebellion is like the sin of divination, and arrogance like the evil of idolatry" (NIV). Satan then has a major foothold in a person's life. That is why most drug addicts or alcoholics fall into sexual sin, lying, deception, and lawlessness.

Other forms of addiction create the same devastation as substance abuse. The pathway to destruction may be different but the end result is the same. All addictions bring a person to spiritual, emotional, physical, and financial bankruptcy. Remember, sin is sin, and all sin leads to death.

Addicts struggle with deep-seated shame. *Shame* is a disturbed or painful feeling of guilt, failure, defect, incompetence, indecency, or blameworthiness. Shame is a deep wounding in our soul that makes us feel we will never be guiltless, worthy of love, or free. The pain of shame cannot be fully described. Some individuals struggle in the depths of shame to the extent that they would rather die than keep on struggling with guilt and shame.

Guilt is the feeling that we have done something wrong that we know is wrong. We are convicted by the Holy Spirit.

False guilt is when we feel guilty, but cannot identify any sin we have committed, or feel guilty for acts, feelings or thoughts that should not produce guilt. Under false guilt, one feels guilty even for other's faults. There is no conviction from the Holy Spirit, but we feel tormented anyway. We feel guilty for no reason.

All addicts struggle with feelings of shame, guilt, and false guilt. Many times the trauma of these feelings is so acute that addicts deny their existence and block out the pain, which results in bondage rather than freedom.

For addicts to become emotionally healed and set free, they must study the Word of God and maintain a prayer life. Then they must take the following steps:

1. Admit that they are addicts and are helpless to stop their behavior.
2. Work through a Christian twelve-step program.
3. Work through all woundedness from childhood. Resolve issues of distrust, judgments, vows, unforgiveness, and lies.
4. Have prayer for any areas of deliverance needed.
5. Be involved in a Christian support group that will call them into accountability when they are exhibiting addictive thinking or behavior.
6. Seek God daily for complete restoration.

When people become addicts, they are living their lives in the flesh rather than in the Spirit. God clearly tells us in His Word that we are not to live according to our flesh. Proverbs teaches us that we are to seek the wisdom of God or we will be foolish. Addicts who refuse to follow God's principles for their lives are fools.

"My son, if you accept my words
and store up my commands within you,
turning your ear to wisdom
and applying your heart to understanding—
indeed, if you call out for insight
and cry aloud for understanding,
and if you look for it as for silver
and search for it as for hidden treasure,
then you will understand the fear of the Lord
and find the knowledge of God.
For the Lord gives wisdom;
from his mouth come knowledge and understanding.
He holds success in store for the upright,
he is a shield to those whose walk is blameless,
for he guards the course of the just
and protects the way of his faithful ones.
Then you will understand what is right and just
and fair—every good path.
For wisdom will enter your heart,
and knowledge will be pleasant to your soul.
Discretion will protect you,
and understanding will guard you.
Wisdom will save you from the ways of wicked men,

from men whose words are perverse,
who have left the straight paths
to walk in dark ways,
who delight in doing wrong
and rejoice in the perverseness of evil,
whose paths are crooked
and who are devious in their ways." (Prov. 2:1-15 NIV)

> "The beginning of wisdom is this: Get wisdom. Though it cost all you have, get understanding. Cherish her, and she will exalt you; embrace her, and she will honor you. She will give you a garland to grace your head and present you with a glorious crown." (Prov. 4:7-9 NIV)

> "My son, pay attention to what I say; turn your ear to my words. Do not let them out of your sight, keep them within your heart; for they are life to those who find them and health to one's whole body. Above all else, guard your heart, for everything you do flows from it. Keep your mouth free of perversity; keep corrupt talk far from your lips. Let your eyes look straight ahead; fix your gaze directly before you. Give careful thought to the paths for your feet and be steadfast in all your ways. Do not turn to the right or the left; keep your foot from evil." (Prov. 4:20-27 NIV)

God clearly shows us throughout the book of Proverbs that when we sin knowingly and repeatedly, we become fools and reap the consequences. Addicts fall into many sinful behavior patterns. As has been previous stated, addicts frequently fall into sins of sex, lying, deception, lawlessness, and deviousness. They become fools because of their sin and rebellion. Let's look at the characteristics of a fool:

The Fool

The book of Proverbs talks about the follies of a fool and equates a fool to being a rebel and wicked. Fools lack common sense. The following are characteristics of a fool according to the book of Proverbs.

Proverbs 26:3, 11-12

- A fool refuses to be taught.
- A fool chooses not to reverence and trust the Lord.
- A fool wants his own way and is complacent, which leads to death.

Proverbs 3:35

- The wise are promoted to honor, but fools are reduced to shame.

Proverbs 6:32

- A man who commits adultery is an utter fool, for he destroys his own soul. Wounds and constant disgrace are his lot.

Proverbs 10:8, 14, 18, 19, 23

- A fool feels self-sufficient and falls flat on his face.
- A fool blurts out everything he knows that only leads to sorrow and trouble.
- To hate is to be a liar; to slander is to be a fool.
- The words of fools are a dime a dozen.
- A fool's fun is in being bad; a wise man's fun is in being wise.

Proverbs 11:12, 29

- To quarrel with a neighbor is foolish.
- The fool who provokes his family to anger and resentment will finally have nothing worthwhile left. He shall be the servant of a wiser man.

Proverbs 12:11, 15, 16, 23

- A fool thinks he needs no advice, but a wise man listens to others.
- A fool is quick-tempered; a wise man stays cool when insulted.
- A wise man doesn't display his knowledge but a fool displays his foolishness.

Proverbs 15:5, 7, 14, 21

- Only a fool despises his father's advice; a wise son considers each suggestion.
- Only the good can give good advice; rebels can't.
- If a man enjoys folly, something is wrong! The sensible persevere on the pathways of right.

Proverbs 18:6, 7; 19:3

- A fool falls into constant fights. His mouth is his undoing! His words endanger him.
- A man ruins his chances by his own foolishness, and then blames the Lord!

Proverbs 20:1-2

- Wine gives false courage; hard liquor leads to brawls; what fools men are to allow it to master them, making them reel drunkenly down the street.

Proverbs 26:4, 11

- When contending with a rebel, don't argue or quarrel as he does or you will become as foolish as he is!
- As a dog returns to his vomit, so a fool repeats his folly.

Proverbs 30:32

- If you have been a fool by being proud or plotting evil, don't brag about it—cover your mouth with your hands in shame.

When you look at some of the characteristics of a fool, do you recognize the same characteristics in addicts? Think about what you have done or the times you have observed the behaviors of addicts and have perceived them as foolish. Addicts often do not recognize their foolishness. They usually try to justify their behavior to others or lie about what they did or did not do. If they do see their sinful attitudes or behaviors, they may minimize or excuse them. Oftentimes, they function from a rebellious heart, which has its roots in wickedness.

What makes a person wise? Proverbs teaches us that the first step to becoming wise is to revere and trust the Lord. One must have a heart that desires to be taught and that seeks after wisdom. God tells us in His Word that if we ask for wisdom, knowledge, and understanding He will give it to us (Prov. 2:6). If we walk in God's wisdom and knowledge with true repentance in our heart when we sin, we will desire to take whatever steps may be required to bring all sinful attitudes of pride, foolishness, rebellion, and wickedness to death on the cross of Jesus Christ. Then, we can ask Christ to give us a new heart and right desires.

When addicts seek God's wisdom and understanding, and begin to bring to death their addictive thinking by the power of the cross, they begin to truly walk out of their addiction. God will restore and renew their mind according to His promises and the power of the Word of God. Their thinking and behavior patterns become new. They truly become "new creatures in Christ."

It is important to realize that when we accepted Jesus as our Lord and Savior by asking Him into our heart, it is at that point that our spirit became new with Him. However, our flesh must be continuously brought to death by applying God's principles in our life. When our sinful fleshly responses and acts are destroyed in us, we become a new creature walking in God's ways.

How do we identify addictive thinking?

- Be informed about what addictive thinking is.
- Identity our addictive behavior—choosing not to be in denial about our behavior and actions.
- Listen to and receive constructive criticism about our behavior.
- Daily do an inventory on our behavior.
- Choose to walk out of our addictive behavior. It is a conscious decision to behave and respond in a way that is uncomfortable and out of the norm for our lifestyle.
- Remember it is an ongoing process. God is consistently renewing our mind as we read His Word and seek Him.

An example of addictive thinking

A young woman who had been off alcohol and drugs for about five years tells the following story:

She was walking into her living room and stubbed her toe on an object lying on the floor. Her four-year-old son was sitting on the floor across the room from her. When she stubbed her toe, she immediately began to blame her son as though he had caused it. Then she caught herself and said, "Wait a minute, my son is across the room. He had nothing to do with stubbing my toe." Her first reaction to blame her son is rooted in an addict's denial system and tendency to blame others for their problems. This woman has worked through much of her addictive thinking and can easily identify when her responses are wrong. Now she corrects her thinking and reacts appropriately.

The Fool Assignment

Go through the list of symptoms of a dysfunctional family. Check those that are characteristic of you. Write them down, and then write what you believe is the root cause of those problems.

How does each characteristic you've checked affect your life?

What sinful behaviors do these characteristics lead you into?

Do you have any addictive behaviors? If so, what are they?

Whom do you blame for your problems?

What do you do to escape facing the responsibility of your sinful behaviors or attitudes?

What "deeds of the flesh" are evident in your life?

What resentments do you have in your heart that hinder you from changing your attitudes and behaviors?

Whom do you have to forgive?

What sins have you committed because of your addictions? Whom have you hurt?

What commandments of God have you broken? Write them down and state how you plan to make restitution for what you have done. Then do it!

How has your addiction hurt you spiritually, emotionally, physically, and financially? Make a list of each of these areas and identify the costs you have paid.

Identify and write down any addictive thought patterns.

Identify your behaviors when you were active in your addictions, and then identify how you might fall into those behaviors now.

Pray through each of the above steps, preferably with someone, asking God's forgiveness for your sins. Break each stronghold and ask God to change your attitudes and behaviors.

Delivered from Pornography Addiction—Testimony

The following is the testimony of a man delivered from pornography.

I suppose my road to pornography addiction started when I was in the fifth grade. We had just moved to a new neighborhood, and I was going to a new school. It just so happened that my dad worked in a large industrial complex that was about a mile away from home. I would go to see him after school. The guys my dad worked with were all Hispanic, younger than my dad, and very foul mouthed. My dad never really cursed, so hearing all the guys around him curse like a sailor was a shock to me.

One day I went to see my dad at work. When I got there, he was really busy and couldn't spend time with me. He had told me to be careful and just look around while he worked. That is when I found the changing room upstairs. What I saw, blew my mind. There were pornographic pictures all over the place—magazines, photographs, cut outs—littering the benches, lockers and bathroom stalls. I had never seen anything like that before. From that moment I found myself always wanting to go back and see more. I never told my dad about seeing the pornography.

Once as I was coming downstairs, he saw me and told me to never go back up there again. He made me promise, but I never kept that promise. Soon after that, I got really busy with school and stopped visiting my dad at work, but I couldn't get the images out of my mind.

Fast forward years later and I was completely addicted. By the time I graduated from high school, I was looking at magazines, videos, and reading erotic books that I bought from an old, used bookstore around the corner from my high school. It wasn't unusual to spend a couple of hours reading and watching the stuff. I had no idea how badly hooked I was.

When I met my wife in my senior year of high school, I figured I could drop the habit, but found it very difficult. I thought that as long as I didn't spend "hours" watching it, I would be okay. Eventually, by the time I graduated high school, I was only into it for about thirty minutes a week. I felt I had beat it, but wasn't sure if I ever could leave it entirely.

A few years down the road, the real impact of pornography became clear to me. I was in chat rooms, talking to different women, watching more hardcore pornography, and feeling completely lost. It controlled me so much that I forgot who I was and I eventually ended up having an affair that nearly destroyed my marriage.

It wasn't until I was at the bottom of the pit that I realized just how badly pornography had ruined who I was as a person. I couldn't go a day without craving it, feeling angry and disgusted, but unable to control the cravings. Around 2011, I met Sydney and she helped me see, through Christ, that I could beat this addiction. I went into counseling, but was really struggling. I wanted to get better, but I was afraid. I don't know why, I just was.

A year after starting counseling, I was able to beat my addiction. To do so, I needed to look at the woundedness in my heart. I discovered that though my dad was physically present in my life, he was emotionally distant and cold. I couldn't share my struggles in any area with my father. How could I talk to a man who never hugged me or told me that he loved me? I can't remember a time after turning eight years old when he told me he cared about me or even loved me.

This was the wound in my heart that Jesus needed to heal. I learned that when I looked at pornography the images sent an adrenaline rush to the limbic part of my brain. That is the part of the brain that records our pain and pleasure. Looking at pornography caused my brain to register pleasure and that covered up pain of not feeling loved by my dad. I had no idea that my addiction was rooted in feeling unloved. In counseling and through the Breaking Free program, Jesus has healed my heart and taken away the pain.

In 2012, I called my dad and confessed everything—the porn and the lack of love I received from him. I had only heard my dad cry twice in his life, but that night as I emptied my heart out to him, he cried. It wasn't the encompassing fix I wanted, but that call led me further down the road of recovery that I desperately wanted and needed.

It took a lot of prayer, working through my woundedness, and love from my wife, but I have obtained victory. I know that I need to faithfully walk with Jesus, be in the Word of God, and trust Him to accomplish in me everything He desires. God is faithful to do that. I praise Him!

Sexual Addiction

Sexual addiction is a sickness and a sin characterized by inappropriate sexual activity. Sin is an addiction. Jesus died on the cross for all of our sinful behavior.

Sexual addicts are no different from alcoholics in that they are trying to control their behavior and failing. They like to think they are in control, but they are not. Their failure to give up control and seek help is what prevents them from coming into healing. *They live a secret life.* They believe they can quit anytime and can do it by themselves. They minimize their sin and refuse to look at their behavior and the consequences of their actions.

Sexual addiction is an escape from feelings. Identifying and dealing with feelings seems too painful or difficult, so they escape through their addictive behavior. Because they did not get affirmation and affection as a child, addicts are constantly searching and trying to get that need in their heart filled by inappropriate sexual behavior.

Addictions lead to unmanageable destructive consequences. Lives, families, careers, and one's spiritual walk with God can be destroyed. God's Word says, "the wages of sin is death" (Rom. 6:23 NIV).

All addicts experience devastating shame and believe they are worthless. Most believe they are failures. Sexual addiction is a sin, and Satan is at work in all addictions. The enemy of our soul creates addictions by using the dynamics of being in unhealthy families, being abused, having deep emotional pain, and devastating feelings of shame, failure, and rejection. Satan wants to convince us we are bad or evil. He sows hopelessness and convinces us to believe we cannot get well. In all addictions, we are at war with the enemy of our soul.

Whether in or out of marriage, sex addicts are lonely individuals who isolate themselves. They may have a large extended family and/or many friends, but no one really knows them. They do not share with others who they are, what they feel, or what they have done. They wear many masks to cover up who they are, or their shame, and even what they really believe about themselves, others, or life in general. It is not unusual for spouses to be unaware of their mate's sexual addiction. A spouse may know there is a problem, but not know what the problem is. When the addiction is brought to light, the spouse then is able to make sense of why problems in the relationship or in the home could never be resolved. Truth was not being brought to light.

Sexual addiction is an infirmity (weakness) which progresses. Behaviors are built progressively. As the adrenaline of one stage loses its thrill, the next worse behavioral step needs to be taken. Behaviors may start very early in the life of the sex addict. The earlier the behaviors start, the harder the addiction is to overcome.

Early building-block stages usually contain masturbation, sexual fantasizing, and use of pornography. Sexual fantasy—thinking about sex—is normally the first step in the addiction. Non-addictive people think about sex and are able to acknowledge the attractiveness of another and then turn their attention elsewhere. A sex addict thinks about sex all the time and has a hard time moving on to other activities. Fantasy can involve remembering past encounters, imagining new ones, or planning how to obtain more sexual encounters. Sex addicts soon don't need to see or be stimulated by pornography in order to fantasize. Any person or situation might trigger sexual thoughts.

Sex therapists teach that fantasizing can be so exciting it causes the body to produce adrenaline, which stimulates and alters one's moods. Fantasy can also stimulate other chemical reactions in the pleasure centers of the brain that positively alter mood and even have a narcotic-like effect. It is like a drug high. Sex addicts use these stimulating highs to escape feelings, to change negative feelings to positive feelings, and to reduce stress. Fantasizing helps to create our own little world.

Pornography frequently is the second stage of addiction. Often, a sex addict is excited about something no one else would find interesting or stimulating. An addict can be excited by a wide variety of written and visual stimuli, ranging from pornographic magazines, videos, TV, movies, strip or peep shows, to bestiality or violent sex. A recovering addict must choose not to participate in sinful activities that trigger sexual addiction.

Pornography opens one's mind to impurity and perversion. The enemy of our soul then has a foothold into one's mind and heart. God's Word says, "But when you follow your own wrong inclinations your lives will produce these evil results: impure thoughts, eagerness for lustful pleasure, idolatry" (Gal. 5:19-20 TLB). Pornography teaches us immoral and unhealthy principles and beliefs about family life, romance, love, relationships, intimacy, and sexuality. If a young person is involved with pornography or often observes it within the family, he/she grows up or enters into marriage having a warped sense of love, intimacy and commitment. Pornography plays a big part in causing an addict to live encased within his/her own isolated little world. When a sex addict, who has learned to isolate himself, marries, the spouse feels unloved, neglected or defiled, and often does not know why. Conflicts develop in the relationship mysteriously. There is no understanding of what the causes are until the addiction is revealed. Fantasy, masturbation, and pornography all work together in a vicious cycle.

Pornography stimulates fantasy.
Fantasy needs to be expressed.
Masturbation allows a release of that need.

The problem with addiction is that need is satisfied only for the moment, negative feelings are not identified or dealt with, and the emotional need and spiritual root deep within the soul are never dealt with. The cycle then continues and more negative feelings develop and shame becomes more deeply ingrained in the heart. This reinforces such beliefs as "I am bad," "I'm a failure," or "I'll never be free." The greater the emotional need, the more rapidly the cycle needs to be repeated. This results in more sexual activity and an increasing downward spiral. This downward spiral may lead to more and more deviant types of sexual behavior such as:

- Involvement with prostitution
- Exhibitionism and voyeurism
- Indecent liberties
- Obscene phone calls
- Rape, incest and child molestation (criminal activity)
- Bestiality

Characteristics of a Sex Addict

The following are some of the typical characteristics of a sex addict:

- They have a poor self-image. They think of themselves as "bad," but put on a front of being superior, acting boastfully, or appearing self-righteous.
- They play a "martyr" role because of perceiving themselves as bad and believe everyone or most people are against them. Or, they play the role of having their life together and everything is going fine.
- They are overachievers or they may be underachievers.

- They may appear to be self-sufficient, but often believe that nobody loves or cares for them.
- They struggle with feelings of rejection, feelings of failure or fear of failure, and feeling unloved or unwanted. They developed these beliefs during childhood.

All of these beliefs can lead to chronic depression, which results in the individual feeling more needy, more isolated, and lonelier. These negative feelings start the addictive cycle all over again.

Sex addicts do not know how to reward themselves in a healthy way or affirm themselves. As the addictive cycle continues, resentment, anger and self-hatred increase. Living with this stress increases stress and negative thoughts of, "I will never be free or I am unable to change." As the stress increases, an addict rewards him/herself by acting out sexually.

Many addicts can go for long periods of time without succumbing to their addictive behavior. Consequently, many sex addicts deny that they are addicted because they have not acted out for an extended period of time. This is only denial. Christian addicts may cover their denial as a spiritual attribute, saying such things as, "I believe my sin is under the blood," or "I am claiming God's healing power." The basis of this kind of denial may actually be a fear of God—belief that they will be punished if the true self is exposed. They may see God as an angry Father who will not set them free, or they may be deceived by believing they are free because they have claimed to be free. Addicts may believe they don't deserve freedom. This is rooted in guilt and shame, not the Word of God. They allow shame to override what the Word of God says.

Relationships

Sex addicts often do not tell those they are afraid of losing about their addiction. They fear that if they tell their loved ones what they are really like and what they have done, they will be abandoned. Therefore, if addicts tell someone, usually it's someone they are not afraid of losing. Unfortunately, addiction usually breaks beyond denial when the addict does something that gets him/her in trouble with the law. How the non-sex addict in the relationship responds when the truth comes out plays a big role in the addict's path to freedom. If the spouse rejects or responds with deep-seated anger, it will hinder the addict looking at truth. The conflict either emotionally closes him/her down or the risk to share feels unsafe.

Sexuality

Sex addicts usually have many sexual experiences, but strangely often know very little about sex. In fact, they may suffer under a lot of misinformation. It is imperative that they learn what God says about sex and what a healthy sexual relationship is within marriage. Three lies addicts usual believe are: (1) casual sex is love, (2) sex will meet my emotional needs, and (3) casual sex is intimacy. Addicts do not have a healthy concept of what love or intimacy is in a marriage. To them, sex is love, but what they have lived is lust.

Most addicts, whether addicted to alcohol, drugs or sex, are afflicted by more than one addiction. They are also quite compulsive and act impulsively without considering the consequences.

Symptoms of Sexual Addiction

- Preoccupation with sexual behaviors.
    - o Pornography
    - o X or R rated movies or videos
    - o Frequent attendance at massage parlors or striptease bars
    - o Conversations center on sex
    - o Uses sexual humor inappropriately
    - o Asks too often for sex or never asks for sex (marriage)

- Escalating patterns of sexual activity.
- Acting distant or withdrawn from loved ones.
- Depression and mood swings. A high after acting out, followed by feelings of shame and repentance.
- Irritability. They do not want to be found out. Questions are uncomfortable for them, and they become defensive.
- Abuse of self or others. If they have been abused as children, they may abuse others in the same way. This could be physical, emotional or sexual. It should be noted that not all who have been abused become abusers, though statistics indicate at least 81% do abuse.
- Resistance to supervision or criticism. They hide their lives so their sin will not be revealed, fearing exposure.
- Use of sexual humor. An innocent statement is often twisted into a sexual content.

- Inappropriate sexual behavior and overt sexual advances. Example: sexual jokes, wandering looks, touching inappropriately, uncomfortable hugs, and direct propositions.
- Family, social, professional, and legal problems. Less time at home, job obligations not met, arrests. etc.

Advice

God has given us intuition, and we must learn to trust it if a spouse feels that something is wrong. It should be investigated. Ignoring what we feel is not a loving response because the addict is slowly spiraling downward. Things will only get worse.

Don't ignore the evidence: charge cards, phone calls with unfamiliar or 900 numbers, pornographic magazines, videos, frequent and unexplained absenteeism from home, gone at unusual hours, etc.

The Unhealthy Family

Recovery from sexual addiction or any other addiction cannot be resolved until the addict understands the woundedness he experienced while growing up in his family. Understanding our unhealthy family dynamics begins the healing process.

The wounded persons must understand:

1. What happened to him/her.
2. That they did not deserve to be abused.
3. That they may not have received the love or nurturing that God intended them to have.
4. That many of the messages they received were incorrect and have become lies within their heart.

Deliverance begins when an addict understands his family dynamics, recognizes how boundaries were violated, understands how rules were verbally and non-verbally communicated, identifies what role he/she played, and what addictions may have been within the biological family.

What makes a family unhealthy?

- Invisible or too rigid boundaries.
- Spoken or unspoken rules that say:

- o We don't talk.
- o We don't feel.
- o We blame others for our problems.
- o We minimize our problems.
- o We deny our problems.

What dysfunctional patterns do couples use to avoid intimacy?

- Repetitive arguments—never resolving issues because it gives partners a screen to avoid dealing with underlying issues.
- Frequently denying or refusing to admit there is a problem in their relationship.
- They can talk about everything except the problems they are encountering in the relationship. On the surface it appears as though they talk a lot, but they don't address their feelings or relationship issues.
- They are involved in many other areas, so they are emotionally depleted to deal with relationship issues. They may do this intentionally.
- They make statements they don't mean or that will deflect the issue that needs to be addressed.
- Criticizing, yelling, finding fault with their spouse over a trivial matter.
- They may take action that they later regret such as shouting profanity, threatening, hitting or throwing things.

In all unhealthy families there are roles individuals assume. Often, an individual within the family may switch roles according to the situation. Common roles are:

1. The Hero (The one who is held in a place of honor or favoritism.)
2. The Scapegoat (The one blamed for all the problems in the family.)
3. The Enabler (The one who care-takes, rescues, or tries to keep peace.)
4. The Mascot (The one who uses humor to ease conflicts--comedians.)
5. The Lost Child (The child who hides or escapes so nobody sees their pain.)
6. The Perfect Child (This child works very hard at being perfect to get approval from others and to eliminate conflict.)

Addictions are rooted in emotional abuse, physical abuse, sexual abuse, and/or spiritual abuse. Pat Carnes found in his research with one thousand sex addicts that 97% were emotionally abused, 74% physically abused, and 81% sexually abused.[9]

Shame

Deep-seated shame resides in every addict. Shame must be healed if one is to come into complete wholeness. Shame is defined by disturbed or painful feelings of guilt, incompetence, or indecency—to hide, to cover, basic sense of covering up. Shame tells us that we do not deserve nor will we ever receive all that God has for us. It is a belief that we probably will not ever be able to earn favor with God. We are hopelessly or irredeemably evil or bad.

Shame causes people to feel as though they want to crawl into a hole and hide. Shame causes its victims to fear exposure of who they believe they are and what sinful behaviors they have committed. Consequently, shame-driven individuals compensate by wearing many masks to prevent exposure of who and what they believe they are. They believe that they can't live up to other people's expectations, so they sabotage relationships. They lie and perform as though they are the kind of person they think others want them to be. This further increases their shame and causes them to push further away from God. The feeling of "unworthiness" thus becomes gigantic, increasing their belief that they are "not worthy of anything good." A shame-driven individual, who has been born again, often believes that "God would not want me because I have ultimately betrayed Him. God won't like me, and I am unworthy of God's blessing."

Shame keeps them from healing and receiving from God or believing His promises. They believe they are unworthy of God's blessings because they will mess up. They see their sin bigger than they can deal with. They feel locked into their sins, unable to comprehend giving them up, being set free, and being forgiven by God and others. It isn't that God can't do it, they don't believe they can do what needs to be done to walk into freedom. They feel powerless.

Shame causes one not to be close to anyone. Shamed people feel disconnected, unlovable, unworthy, and deeply different from others. The shame-driven person believes people see him/her as worse than he/she really is. Shame-filled individuals suffer warped perceptions and are consumed by other's thoughts about them. Being consumed by what people think helps them hide from their feelings of shame. If they are not thinking about what others think of them, their defenses are down, and they have to look at their sin. It is a frightening process when sins are exposed, particularly since they have lived in rebellion their entire life in order to prevent the shame from being exposed. Shame from sin can penetrate so deeply that the victim becomes hardened to other sinful activities. Shame makes one compromise values. There is often the feeling, "What more can I feel? How can I feel worse?" Violating self becomes "no big deal."

To be released from feelings of shame we must first:

- Commit our life to Christ and be obedient to His Word.
- Admit there is shame.
- Deal with our sin that resulted in us having shame.
- Walk a pure and righteous life.
- Commit ourselves to getting our heart healed.
- Receive healing prayer.
- Understand that Jesus took our shame on the cross.

Understanding and appropriating what Jesus accomplished on the cross will free us of shame. To walk into that freedom, one must first look at the woundedness in the heart to know what must be given to Jesus and healed. We can know in our head what Jesus has done for us, but not have it within our heart. Isaiah 61:1 says that Jesus would be sent "to bind up the brokenhearted, to proclaim freedom for the captives" (NIV).

Sex addicts are not terrible, immoral people. Many hate their sin and hate themselves for what they do. The devil uses lust to lead them astray because of their woundedness. Their sexual acting out has mainly been a survival technique. Their acting out may lessen their pain, but it is a slow sure path to death. Proverbs 14:12 says, "There is a way *that seems* right to a man, But its end *is* the way of death" (NKJV). They are dying inside emotionally and spiritually. They must learn to give up their coping mechanisms to walk out of their addiction. To do so means they are giving up on the strategy they believe has kept them functioning.

Counselors working with addicts must work with the adult who wants freedom and the child within who does not want it because of fear.

Healing

There are many steps in the healing process. First is the recognition by addicts that they need help and that they cannot overcome their problems by themselves. They are powerless to overcome their sin. Second is that addicts must be willing to become very honest. Dishonesty and lying have kept them from looking at their sin. God's Word says "the truth will set you free" (John 8:32 NIV). There needs to be a total surrender to God.

The next step is to earnestly look at the woundedness that took place during childhood. Hebrews 12:15 says, "See to it that no one falls short of the grace of God and that no bitter root grows up to cause trouble and defile many" (NIV). Addicts needs to look at the bitter roots and judgments that were planted there when they were children. Cleansing prayer and forgiveness need to be applied to inner wounding.

When possible, an addict needs to make amends to those he/she has defiled or wounded. He/she needs to ask for forgiveness for sinning against them. The addict needs to come before the Lord and ask God to reveal his/her shortcomings and any sinful attitudes or behaviors that need to be brought to death. In the process of all this, the addict needs to:

1. Stop the sexual behaviors.
2. Stop the sexual rituals.
3. Stop the fantasizing.
4. Allow anger to surface.
5. Grieve over loses.
6. Set up healthy boundaries.
7. Learn how to play.
8. Seek professional help or a sexual addiction support group.

Healing from addiction is a spiritual journey. There may be times in which we slip or relapse. We shouldn't beat ourselves up. If we continue in the healing process, we will walk into victory.

Marriage

Addicts usually are co-dependent and have a tendency to marry someone who is also co-dependent or addictive. Part of the healing process in the marriage is to be honest with one another and begin to learn what intimacy really is within a marriage. Intimacy is developed when both partners risk telling each other who they really are, how they feel, and what they are thinking. Truth always builds intimacy. When truth is revealed, trust begins to develop in the relationship, which makes the co-addict begin to feel safe. That person then has an understanding of what the other is thinking or feeling and doesn't feel threatened that the addict is going to return into denial and addictive behaviors. If the addict is acting out and honestly shares this with the spouse, the truth can help them work together on the problem—providing the spouse is not co-dependently dismissing or excusing inappropriate behaviors. Looking at the sin and working together to obtain victory is progress.

Intimacy is further developed when couples learn to resolve problems in a healthy way. Previous attempts to resolve conflicts may have included fighting, deception, extra-marital affairs, lying, silence treatment, punishment, isolation, sexual unavailability, and character assassination. As truth is shared and intimacy develops, this leads the addict into unfamiliar territory. This is uncomfortable because it is new and different. There is a tendency to fall back into old behavior patterns. We are to resist the temptation, ask God to strengthen and help us be obedient to follow His guidelines for marriage (James 4:7). This is an upward struggle, but obedience produces quality fruit.

Many couples believe divorce is the answer to their problems. This is far from the truth. The wounds and behaviors learned by both the addict and co-addict do not go away when divorce happens. Learned dysfunctionality continues into the next relationships. Healing of relationships needs to happen while in the relationship. We cannot heal a relationship when we are by ourselves. God says, "He will restore us." Allow Him to do it.

The only exception to the above may be if the addict refuses to get help, someone is being abused, and it is dangerous to stay. If this is the situation, we are to seek wise godly counsel for direction.

Remember, this is a spiritual journey. The couple who prays together, reads the Word together, and attends church together is a couple who will walk into healing and restoration.

> "Don't look to men for help; their greatest leaders fail; for every man must die. His breathing stops, life ends, and in a moment all he planned for himself is ended. But, happy is the man who has the God of Jacob as his helper, whose hope is in the Lord his God - the God who made both earth and heaven, the seas and everything in them. HE IS THE GOD WHO KEEPS EVERY PROMISE, and gives justice to the poor and oppressed, and food to the hungry. He frees the prisoners, and opens the eyes of the blind; he lifts the burdens from those bent down beneath their loads. For the Lord loves good men." (Ps. 146:3-8 TLB)

> "The Lord lifts the fallen and those bent beneath their load ... The Lord is fair in everything he does, and full of kindness. He is close to all who call on him sincerely. He fulfills the desires of those who reverence and

trust him; he hears their cries for help and rescues them. He protects all those who love him, but destroys the wicked." (Ps. 145:14, 17-20 TLB)

"Hear my prayer, O Lord; answer my plea, because you are faithful to your promises ... Bring me out of all this trouble because you are true to your promises." (Ps. 143:1, 11 TLB)

"Lord, if you keep in mind our sins then who can ever get an answer to his prayers? But you forgive! What an awesome thing this is! That is why I wait expectantly, trusting God to help, for He has promised." (Ps. 130:3-5 TLB)

Characteristics of a Sex Addict Assignment

If you struggle with sexual addiction, identify the areas of woundedness from your childhood. Write down everything you have done that causes you to feel deep shame.

Go back to the section on belief systems and identify what you learned to believe about yourself when you were a child.

Write down your beliefs and find scriptures that counter the untruths you have believed.

Identify your cycle of sexual acting out. What stresses, feeling, etc... started you on your addictive cycle?

Write your cycle down.

Identify how you use blame and denial to justify your behaviors.

Learn to recognize how you manipulate and control others. Ask those close to you to help you recognize when you are controlling and/or manipulating. Journal about what you do.

Identify how you lie to yourself and others to cover up your shame and/or sin.

Identify how and when you isolate yourself. Choose not to allow yourself to become isolated under any circumstance. Communicate what you are struggling with or feeling to an individual to whom you can be accountable.

Have someone you trust, and is anointed by God, pray for your healing and deliverance as many times as needed until you are free.

If your addiction is longstanding, get into a support group that will help you work through the addiction. **REMEMBER, DON'T GIVE UP. GOD AND YOU CAN DO IT!**

Anger Was Destroying Me—Testimony

The testimony written below is by a couple who struggled with anger and control. Their marriage was almost destroyed until they learned how to apply the biblical principles taught in this manual.

The Wife's Story

This was a second marriage for both of us. As is typical of all marriages, each of us had brought emotional baggage from our past into our marriage. We had already been to a number of Christian counselors and none of them had been able to help us.

I was full of anger, rage, resentment and hate. I knew some of the reasons I was angry, but not all. I had no idea how much or how deep my anger went. It was so bad that when I tried to do something nice it always came out wrong. When my son died, things got even worse. I became more angry, resentful, and hateful because I believed that my husband and his boys contributed to my son's death. In the outside world I was usually able to keep my anger in check, but at home it was a different situation. I was a walking battle zone. Anger and rage spilled out on anyone who looked at me cross-eyed! One counselor said that I had the same kind of background as his wife, and he could sympathize. He stated that most of the problems in the marriage were because of me. Every time I left this counselor's office I cried as I felt I was to blame for everything. He had absolutely no understanding of what was happening to me. He just increased my anger and resentment of men. Another counselor questioned my Christianity and told me that if I was serious I needed to do something. I asked her what and how. I was willing to do anything because I knew I needed help. She just told me "do it." I am one of those people you either have to show or tell how to do something. When she said "just do it," I became very angry and resentful. I terminated counseling with her.

Through individual counseling with Sydney and using the Breaking Free teaching, I came to understand why I was so angry and how to deal with the anger. The main thing I needed to do was forgive those who had hurt me through the years. I had been terribly abused as a child and in my first marriage. I had never dealt with what such abuse had done to me emotionally and spiritually. Through journaling I was able to grasp why I was so angry. Then, I was taught I had to forgive everyone who had hurt me. It did not matter whether the hurt was real or perceived. I had to forgive. In some cases I actually went to the person and asked for forgiveness for the attitudes in my heart toward them. For those with whom it is not practical or possible to talk with to ask forgiveness, I just asked God to be in that situation. Through the teaching I began to deal with each area in which I had a problem. There were many events in my life about which I was angry. We prayed through each of them, and I received my healing.

My rage is totally gone. I occasionally get angry, but that comes and goes normally, as with most people. I no longer carry grudges. My resentments are simply gone. My husband has noticed a big difference in me, and he likes it. In fact, he started to notice a difference within the first few counseling sessions. I was looking for help and found someone who was willing to teach me how to be free instead of saying "just do it."

When I was able to rid myself of the rage, anger and resentment, my countenance changed. I went from someone whose facial features appeared hard and angry to someone whose countenance is much softer and more peaceful. I have peace within me that I never believed possible. Inside I am at peace with the world and myself. My marriage is better, and we are starting to grow closer. As I move towards completing the healing process, I look forward with joyful hope to the type of life and marriage that God intended His children to have. I am at peace.

The Husband's Response

Sydney's teaching on spiritual principles saved our marriage and set us free. We did not know how our anger and controlling behaviors could be healed, or even where those behaviors came from. Through the series of teachings on belief systems, strongholds, judgments, expectancies and other principles, we were able to understand the causes of our problems. Prayer for deliverance and commitment to change released us from bondage. Anyone serious enough to put effort into learning these principles and acting on them can be set free.

Anger

Anger is rooted in pain. Individuals who have problems with anger have not learned how to handle offenses or how to release pain and hurt to the Lord. They have held their feelings inside without expressing to those who have offended them what they are thinking or feeling. Failure to deal with offenses or pain causes one's anger to build until some form of explosion takes place. Most adults who have serious anger problems have never been healed of hurts and wounds from their childhood. They have hidden pain within their heart, believing or hoping it will go away. Unfortunately, roots of resentment, bitterness, hatred, and unforgiveness do not just go away. Such roots produce present misdirected anger, rage and hatred. God's Word clearly describes repercussions produced by anger in one's life. It is the mishandling of anger that can become sinful. Paul commanded, "In your anger do not sin" (Eph. 4:26 NIV).

> "Your own soul is nourished when you are kind; it is destroyed when you are cruel ... The fool who provokes his family to anger and resentment will finally have nothing worthwhile left. He shall be the servant of a wiser man." (Prov. 11:17, 29 TLB)

> "Keep away from angry, short-tempered men, lest you learn to be like them and endanger your soul." (Prov. 22:24 TLB)

> "There is more hope for a fool than for a man of quick temper." (Prov. 29:20 TLB)

It is important to realize that what is in our heart will be what comes out of our mouth.

> "But the things that come out of a person's mouth come from the heart, and these defile them. For out of the heart come evil thoughts—murder, adultery, sexual immorality, theft, false testimony, slander. These are what defile a person; but eating with unwashed hands does not defile them." (Matt. 15:18-20 NIV)

> "But I tell you that everyone will have to give account on the day of judgment for every empty word they have spoken. For by your words you will be acquitted, and by your words you will be condemned." (Matt. 12:36-37 NIV)

God has given each person free will to choose what to do with anger. Each individual must choose how to deal with anger. Angry people tend to blame others for the consequences of their own sins rather than learn to take responsibility and deal with their own anger. Anger is an emotion that should not be allowed to control us. We are to control our anger. We do not have to become a habitually angry person.

In many individuals, problems with anger began during childhood or early adolescence. Inappropriate ways of handling anger developed as a result of wounds caused by feeling unappreciated, belittled, taken for granted, helpless, or in some way insignificant. Appropriate ways to channel the anger were not developed. Anger begins with the offense. Rather than expressing our feelings, we tend to let emotions escalate within us for so long that when feelings are expressed they are said in hurtful and sometimes aggressive ways. Repeatedly handling our anger in this way will result in developing patterns of communication that are very destructive to ourselves and others.

As stated, roots of anger usually come from childhood. Children need to learn to be responsible and to do their best. However, when performance is required and feelings are ignored, a child learns that feelings do not matter. This kind of message placed upon a child slowly causes her/him to feel bitter. The child begins to feel unacceptable "as is" and finds acceptance only for what he/she does. When the child entertains these feelings repeatedly, anger increases with feelings of bitterness, resentment and rebellion. As a result of these feelings, the child has a difficult time developing trust. Bitter-root judgments, bitter-root expectancies, and inner vows are now in operation in life. Hebrews 12:15 says, "See to it that no one falls short of the grace of God and that no bitter root grows up to cause trouble and defile many" (NIV).

As time passes, other circumstances in life reinforce the messages the child has believed, resulting in increased anger. Many adults who have struggled with anger since childhood grow up to be physically, emotionally or sexually abusive to others.

They have developed a belief system and behavior patterns that are destructive to themselves and others. One of the character flaws that develops because of anger is the need and desire to have power and control over others. A basic belief—subconscious or conscious—is if they are not in control, they are out of control and life will not go well for them.

Many times, the anger and need to have power and control are learned by what children have observed in their parents as they were growing up. Sadly, when the anger is rooted in childhood not only has the child learned negative destructive ways, but the child has never learned wholesome appropriate behavior. Such children have not learned how to solve problems effectively. Instead, they often try to solve problems by becoming angry, leaving, or controlling others. They develop defense mechanisms that prevent them from working through their problems, which would require them to examine what they are feeling and acknowledge and deal with their pain. This is foreign behavior to them. Therefore, conflict resolution has not become an alternative—they just react.

Our society today has badly abused the emotion of anger to the point of self-destruction and destruction in the family. We live in a society that has become accustomed to people's angry outbursts. We often hear the statement: "I have a right to be angry." Anger may be justified, but how a person responds in anger to others may be totally unacceptable. Oftentimes, anger is used for selfish gain. People want things their own way.

Anger produces fleshly rewards such as power, feelings of superiority, intimidation, emotional distance, and the ability to manipulate and control. People have become skilled in covering up anger by using such words as *anxious, bored, depressed, frustrated, grieved, upset* or *stressed-out.* Our society has embraced and accepted such excuses too readily.

By expressing anger, individuals are:

- Trying to stand up for themselves.
- Inappropriately stating they deserve to be treated better.
- Trying to express that they have worth.
- Saying "notice my needs."
- Trying to get respect.

Characteristics of Angry People

- They are stubborn and unyielding.
- They feel insecure, vulnerable and unloved.
- They manipulate and control.
- They fear being open or intimate with people.
- They do not trust people.
- They will not take "no" for an answer.
- They want their own way.
- They are aggressive and demanding.
- They are non-compromising, seeing issues as black or white.
- They use key words for control such as *have to, must, ought to, should, supposed to, you'd better.*
- They may use guilt or condemnation.
- They may be perfectionists or the opposite, not performing necessary tasks.
- They are rebellious and foolish.
- They are selfish and spoiled.
- They struggle with feelings of rejection and failure or fear of failure.
- They may procrastinate by saying they forgot or just not doing what is needed to be done.

Reactive angry people often become abusive to others, especially those who are close to them. They may try to abuse or gain control of others by using any number of the following:

- **Isolation:** Controlling what others do, who they see and talk to, where they go.
- **Intimidation:** Putting people in fear by using looks, actions, gestures, loud voices, destroying property.
- **Emotional Abuse:** Putting people down or making them feel bad about themselves, name calling, playing mind games, making them think they are crazy.
- **Economic Abuse:** Trying to keep a person from getting or keeping a job. Making her/him ask for money, giving an allowance, but taking back the money.
- **Sexual Abuse:** Making people do sexual things against their will. Physically attacking the sexual parts of the body. Treating people like sex objects.
- **Threats:** Making or carrying out threats to cause harm. Threatening to take the children, commit suicide, report her/him to welfare.

- **Using Children:** Making her/him feel guilty about the children, using the children to give messages, using visitation as a way to harass.
- **Physically:** Twisting arms, tripping, biting, pushing, shoving, hitting, punching, kicking, grabbing, pulling hair, choking, slapping, beating, using a weapon, throwing a person down.
- **Silent Treatment:** Refusing to communicate by being silent. It is the most controlling use of anger. Silence is a way of saying, "You are not worthy enough to talk to." The message is always one of strong disapproval. The person receiving the silent treatment has no way of fighting back, which creates further irritation and conflict. Angry people increase their own bitterness by being silent.

Anger in Marriage

Unresolved anger in our marriage will destroy our relationship and our love for each other. Angcr is a learned behavior and when manifested in our life will cause us to walk in sin and result in iniquity for our children. Parents have the most profound influence on their children. Children need to see how to resolve conflict. If they don't learn it as children, they will have difficulty or not be able to resolve conflict in their relationships or marriage.

The enemy of our soul, Satan, wants to destroy marriages. If he is successful, he has not only destroyed the marriage and the family, but he has hurt the body of Christ. How does the enemy of our soul work? He works with our unresolved sin issues such as bitterness, unforgiveness, unrepentance, and lies we believe about ourselves, others and God. In the Word of God, our enemy is called the accuser of the brethren. He is the accuser, a liar and a slander. His goal is to destroy us.

We must submit ourselves to God in obedience or the enemy gets a foothold in our life.

> "Submit yourselves, then, to God. Resist the devil, and he will flee from you. Come near to God and he will come near to you. Wash your hands, you sinners, and purify your hearts, you double-minded." (James 4:7-8 NIV)

The devil lies to us by attempting to convince us that our wrong behavior will bring good results. For example, one lie is expecting change by yelling at a spouse and telling him/her how wrong they are and what they need to change or do. The yelling and anger only result in our spouse resisting us or closing their heart.

Another way the devil tries to get us off track is by convincing us that no matter what we do, nothing will change. When we listen to this lie, we are tempted to fall into another lie that our spouse doesn't care or their motives are destructive or evil toward us. Then, the devil will put these thoughts into our head:

- I married the wrong person.
- I made a mistake, and I'm not in love anymore.
- My spouse is not the right person for me.

We will also accuse our spouse of future actions that have not been committed. Unresolved anger gives the devil permission to come in and say or do what he wants. Anger is not just an emotion, but a whole system of thoughts. That is why God says in His Word that we need to "demolish arguments and every pretension that sets itself up against the knowledge of God, and we take captive every thought to make it obedient to Christ" (2 Cor. 10:5 NIV).

There are many reasons a person gets angry. Some individuals have been angry since childhood because of their life circumstances. Others get angry because:

- They feel their boundaries have been crossed.
- They feel they are not being listened to or they are misunderstood.
- They are immature and have not learned to look at a situation from various points of view.
- They have unrealistic expectations of their spouse.
- They feel it's their spouse's responsibility to meet all their needs.
- They feel that if their spouse complains about something they are being rejected or are a failure.
- They feel disrespected and not valued.
- They have woundedness in their heart that has not been healed. When a spouse says or does something that touches that wound, they react in anger.

When anger is easily exhibited, the atmosphere in the home does not feel safe. A spouse needs to know that he/she can share anything without having to pay a price. If the situation is such that a person does not feel safe, they often will close down and not talk, or they will give the spouse the silent treatment. That is not healthy either. Silent treatment gives the message that the other person is not valued or worth talking too. Individuals that have a tendency to be abusive will frequently use the silent treatment. They may go days without speaking to their spouse. This is one of the worst forms of abuse.

Dysfunctional families don't talk or share their feelings. Intimacy cannot develop in a marriage without feelings being shared. Intimacy is the glue that holds a marriage together. A healthy marriage has anger, and it gets resolved without wounding each other. An unhealthy marriage is when anger is held in and then erupts. Anger will kill intimacy and often results in a person developing a "stony heart" toward their spouse. When a spouse says they are "out of love," that is anger. Once they work through their issues and learn to talk through and share their feelings, the love ignites in their heart again. Unfortunately, many couples do not work on developing intimacy, but rather choose divorce.

Some of the causes for divorce are:

- Unforgiveness
- Bitterness
- Critical spirit - putting the other person down or never showing approval of what they say or do.
- Control and domination – things have to be your way, decisions are made by you and the family is to obey and follow. Control may be over money, children, sex, friends, and family activities.
- Defensiveness – defending your thoughts or decisions on a regular basis.
- Anger – can be rage, silent treatment, verbal abuse, emotional abuse, physical abuse or sexual abuse.
- Lack of intimacy – this may be exhibited by a couple living in the same house, but never sharing their feelings or thoughts with each other.
- Affair – very damaging to each person in the marriage. The pain and wounds of that can last for years and are usually carried into a future marriage.

In a healthy home, the husband is the spiritual leader and he treats his wife as an equal. He initiates the well-being of the home. He leads, not dominates. A woman wants her husband to lead. When he leads, she feels very safe and protected. A husband that daily prays over his wife will see the blessings of the Lord in his home. His wife will cherish her husband and will stand beside him no matter what life tosses at them. God made the wife to be her husband's help-mate. A woman's heart is to support and stand by her husband. However, if the husband doesn't love, protect, and spiritually lead her as Christ has told him to, the women's heart often disconnects from her husband, and she loses respect for him.

> "Submit to one another out of reverence for Christ. Wives, submit yourselves to your own husbands as you do to the Lord. For the husband is the head of the wife as Christ is the head of the church, his body, of which he is the Savior. Now as the church submits to Christ, so also wives should submit to their husbands in everything. Husbands, love your wives, just as Christ loved the church and gave himself up for her to make her holy, cleansing her by the washing with water through the word and to present her to himself as a radiant church, without stain or wrinkle or any other blemish but holy and blameless. In the same way, husbands ought to love their wives as their own bodies. He who loves his wife loves himself. After all, no one ever hated their own body, but they feed and care for their body, just as Christ does the church for we are all members of his body." (Eph. 5:21-30 NIV)

It is interesting to note that God did not tell the wife to love her husband. He told the husband to love his wife. A woman has been given a heart by the Lord to just naturally love. If she feels loved by her husband, she will respect him. A man feels valued if he receives respect and admiration from his wife.

Pastor Jimmy Evans states there are four foundational laws of marriage.[10] He states those four laws are:

1. **The Law of Independence:** Leave your father and mother. Marriage is about inter-independence. Marriage only works when your spouse is in first place in your life. Jealousy in marriage is natural. When children come, parents become protective. But a spouse belongs to you first. A spouse will get jealous if not in first place in your life. When not placed first, women become attentive to children and men turn to their career.
2. **The Law of Protection:** Protect your relationship. Don't allow people or activities into your relationship that will cause conflict or trouble. A prenuptial is damaging as it starts your marriage with no trust.
3. **The Law of Purity:** Be careful about what you do. After the fall, man began to hide from others and God (fig leaves). When living marriage in purity, you can expose your differences and talk about sensitive issues without a problem. When there is the sin of impurity in your marriage, there is distrust and you can't talk about sensitive issues. Intimacy is damaged.

4. **The Law of Possession:** Never act without your spouse's approval. You share everything, and there is no sense of "mine and yours." The joy of marriage is sharing and doing things together.

Christ teaches us to be servants to one another and to be sacrificial. In a healthy relationship, we should be asking ourselves what we can and should give up for our spouse.

> "Jesus called them together and said, 'You know that the rulers of the Gentiles lord it over them, and their high officials exercise authority over them. Not so with you. Instead, whoever wants to become great among you must be your servant, and whoever wants to be first must be your slave—just as the Son of Man did not come to be served but to serve, and to give his life as a ransom for many.'" (Matt. 20:25-28 NIV)

We need to have a Christ-like servant heart and attitude that says:

- I will sacrifice the belief that you need to give up something for me.
- I will give you my time, which says, "You are important to me."
- I will eliminate things or activities that are perceived to be more important than our relationship.
- I will make any changes in my life that I need to make that will affirm that you are the most important priority in my life.
- I will confirm to you that I will do whatever it takes to prove that you are number one in my life.

There is no question that committing and making sacrificial changes in our life to improve one's marriage can be hard, but the rewards far outweigh the sacrifice. Anger produces death in a relationship, a servant's heart produces love, joy, peace and a fulfilled marriage relationship. Aim for all God has. Don't settle for less as destruction is often the fruit of that decision.

Anger in Marriage Assignment

What effort have you made in your marriage to develop intimacy in your relationship?

List what you have done.

What struggles do you have regarding intimacy?

What are you afraid of if you emotionally open yourself up to your spouse and share your feelings, fears, pain and struggles?

What behaviors do you need to change?

What steps are you going to take to develop intimacy?

Fighting Behaviors

Escalation: Escalation occurs when we say or do something negative, our spouse responds with something negative, and the fight starts. The result is to become increasingly angry and hostile as the argument continues. Answer the following questions:

1. How often do you think you escalate arguments as a couple?

2. Do you get hostile with each other during escalation?

3. What or who usually brings an end to the fight?

4. Do one or the other of you sometimes threaten to end the relationship when angry?

5. How do each of you feel when you are escalating as a couple? Do you feel tense, anxious, scared, angry, or something else?

Invalidation: Invalidation occurs when you subtly or directly put down the thoughts, feelings, actions or worth of your spouse. This is different from simply disagreeing with your spouse or not liking something he or she has done. Invalidation includes belittling or disregarding what is important to your spouse out of insensitivity or outright contempt. Ask yourself these questions and look at your attitude and behaviors.

1. Do you often feel invalidated in your relationship? When and how does this happen?

2. What is the effect on you?

3. Do you often invalidate your spouse? When and how does this happen?

4. What do you think the effect is on him or her? On the relationship? What are you trying to accomplish when you do this? Do you accomplish that goal?

Withdrawal and Avoidance: Ask yourself these questions and look at your attitude and behaviors.

1. Is one of you more likely to be the pursuer and one of you play the withdrawer role? If you are the withdrawer, how do you withdraw? If you are the pursuer, how do you pursue?

2. When are you most likely to fall into this pattern as a couple? Are there particular issues or situations that bring out this behavior?

3. How are you affected by these behavioral responses?

4. For some couples, either or both partners tend to pursue or both tend to withdraw at the same time. Is this true in your marriage? If so, why do you think this happens?

Negative Interpretations: Ask yourself these questions and look at your attitude and behaviors.

1. Can you think of some circumstances where you see your spouse's behavior as negative? What are the advantages to you in making these interpretations?

2. As you reflect on this, do you really think your negative view of your spouse's behavior is justified?

3. Are you open to considering that you may be missing information that would present a different view of the situation?

4. List two or three issues where you are willing to challenge yourself to look for the possibility that your spouse has a more positive motivation than you have been thinking he/she has. Identify any evidence that is contrary to your interpretation.

All conflict starts with the enemy working in our life with the goal of destroying or hindering our walk and relationship with the Lord, destroying our marriage, hurting and doing emotional damage to our children, and ultimately hurting the reputation of the body of Christ. To get victory, we need to know and understand how the enemy of our soul, Satan, works. Below are some of his tactics.

What is the enemy like?

- Deceptive
- Cunning
- Liar
- Bondage maker
- Knows our weaknesses
- Afflicts wounds
- Knows how to strategically attack us

- Entices disobedience in us
- Utilizes circumstances to bring us into unbelief, distrust and fear
- Reopens old wounds convincing us of the lies he gives us, resulting in closing our heart to God and others
- Brings conflict/crisis to lead us away from God's truths and principals
- Destroys foundation of relationship: love, honor and trust

How does the enemy use us?

- We speak words that hurt or curse others.
- We withhold love, affection and intimacy.
- We blame our spouse rather than be accountable/responsible for our own wrong behavior.
- We ignore each other and get our needs met elsewhere.
- We fail to show deep, honest feelings, but will express anger.
- We choose to not be honest with each other or ourselves.
- We exhibit verbal or physical abuse.
- We are controlling and domineering.

How do we fight the enemy?

By recognizing and knowing the enemy's strategy to cause conflict in the marriage. The enemy will:

- Use unhealed wounds to develop unhealthy emotional and behavioral responses such as withholding love, affection and intimacy. He will feed into our minds unrealistic expectations and a faulty belief system about our spouse, others, and ourselves. We react by what we imagine in our mind that our spouse is thinking and feeling.
- Influence us to respond to hurts and conflicts in the flesh rather than being led by the Spirit.
- Influence us to deny problems exist in the relationship.
- Influence us to make statements we don't mean or to deflect the issue at hand.
- Influence us to criticize our spouse or find fault with him/her over a trivial matter.
- Influence us to take action we regret such as shouting profanity or hitting and throwing things.

- Tempt us to argue repetitively over the same issues, never resolving the real underlying issue.
- Cause us to become emotionally depleted.

When conflict arises it is important to know how to fight without wounding each other. Every marriage has conflict, but heathy marriages have learned how to effectively fight in a godly manner.

Healthy Fighting

Healthy fighting requires setting up healthy guidelines for working through and resolving issues when we are angry. Here are some suggested ideas:

- Develop fighting rules and a contract
- Agree on the fight
- Agree on a time and place to fight
- Set some time limits to fights
- Fight in the presence of a third party if you don't feel safe

When fighting, agree to not:

- Fight in front of children
- Blame
- Swear
- Use "you" statements
- Try to out-yell one another
- Hit or threaten to hit
- Throw things
- Argue in inappropriate places
- Name call
- Case build (use the past to support your case)
- Button-push (mention known sensitive areas)
- Temporarily exit the relationship (emotionally or physically)

Write up a contract between you and your spouse on how you are going to respond to each other when in conflict. Follow it faithfully and see the Lord's blessings in your marriage. It will knit your hearts together.

The following is an example of a contract one couple drew up. They have seen their conflict level decrease dramatically as a result.

RULES OF ENGAGEMENT (FIGHT CONTRACT)

AGREEMENT FOR PEACEFUL RESULTS WHEN DISAGREEMENTS OCCUR IN OUR MARRIAGE

We will keep the environment safe (loving, caring and accepting) at all times by:

- Beginning with prayer.
- Showing honor and respect for each other.
- Honestly sharing our feelings.
- Actively and carefully listening to each other.
- Using softened tones.
- Using humor.
- Asking if my perception (as explained) is accurate.
- Stepping back and waiting to engage when calmer.
- Believing the best of each other.
- Acknowledging each other's point of view.
- Retaining the goal to "know (understand) and be known" by each other (sharing our hearts).
- Walking in unity, recognizing and honoring our differences.
- Asking the question, "Did I hear and/or understand you correctly?"
- Committing to humble ourselves before God and each other.
- Recognizing the enemy's tactics and not succumbing to them.

We will then each read out loud to one another the following scriptures:

- Ephesians 4:2-3
- Colossians 3:12-15
- 1 Corinthians 13:4-7

We agree to NOT:

- Blame
- Use "you" statements
- Swear
- Roll our eyes
- Yell or raise voices
- Threaten, pursue or leave
- Use the past or bring in the past
- Mention known sensitivities
- Exit mentally
- Continue longer than 15 minutes without a break

At every break and at the finish we will pray.

We agree to the above contract and with God's help we will resolve conflict in a godly way.

Name: ______________________________ Date: ______________

Name: ______________________________ Date: ______________

Rules for a Healthy Relationship

- It is okay to feel.
- It is okay to have conflict, just do it in a healthy way.
- It is okay to have needs, but realize that your spouse will not meet all your needs.
- Respect your partner. No self-righteous statements.
- No bating or button-pushing.
- No case-building (you did this, or this, or this)
- No taking each other's inventory.
- Respect yourself – be aware of the times and how your put yourself down. Try to build yourself up.
- Take responsibility for your story – the actions and consequences of your past.
- No self-pity – don't get stuck in the victim role. You are in the victim role if you experience ongoing anger.
- What you and your spouse share needs to be kept confidential.
- Rid yourself of expectations. "Expectations are premediated resentments."

Dysfunctional Patterns Couples Use to Avoid Intimacy

- Repetitive arguments – never resolving the issues because it gives partner a screen to avoid dealing with the underlying issues.
- Frequent periods of denial – refusing to admit problems in the relationship.
- Nonproductive communications – can talk about everything except the problems they face. On the surface it appears as though they talk a lot, but not about feelings regarding relationship issues.
- Extension and depletion – emotionally depleted. Too involved in other areas.
- Making statements you don't mean. Making statements that deflect the issue at hand such as criticizing your spouse or finding fault with him/her over a trivial matter.
- Taking action you regret such as shouting profanity or hitting and throwing things. True intimacy is avoided.

Circle the issues which trouble your relationship:

- Sex
- Roles
- Controlling partner's "mistakes"
- Money
- Trust
- Partner's family
- Kids
- Past behaviors
- Unfair fighting
- Separate issues

THE ABUSE CYCLE

When abuse happens in a home, it is important for abused individuals to be able to recognize the cycle of violence. There are three stages to the cycle of abuse. The first is the tension building stage, then acute explosion, and then the honeymoon stage. (See the chart to identify the characteristics of each stage.). It is important to realize that as time goes on, each cycle is repeated more frequently. For example, an individual may have only one or two explosions a year, then increase to four or five, and eventually augment to weekly or even daily explosions. The intensity and frequency of abuse continues to increase until the cycle is broken or stopped. Victims of abuse are increasingly more emotionally, spiritually, and possibly physically damaged. Victims often blame themselves for what is happening to them and the family. They may say, "If I could only do things better he/she would not get so mad." Victims may also believe they are going "crazy." Only by breaking through the abuser's denial system and making them look at their behavior and belief system can the cycle be broken. Above all else, victims of abuse must be protected and, if necessary, enabled to leave the abusive situation.

Getting free of anger and abusive behavior requires becoming thoroughly honest with God, others and ourselves. We must be willing to see how we have hurt others and recognize the consequences of our behavior. We need to take full responsibility for our actions. We must not blame others for our behavior. Angry individuals have a tendency to blame others for their mistakes and any consequences they have to suffer because of their sins. Individuals possessed by deep-seeded anger need professional counseling.

Depression is another result of repressed anger. There are many reasons a person becomes depressed. We will only discuss the problems of depression due to unresolved anger. Depression is a passive way of communicating that a person cannot measure up to demands or the world doesn't measure up to expectations. It can be an act of aggression if the depressed person is withdrawing from others. In such cases, such people are falling into self-pity and do not want to take on unwanted responsibilities. This is not true of all who fall into depression.

Biblical View of Anger

The primary reason God created mankind was so that we could know His love. God has given us the capability of both giving and receiving love. We are created in the image of God (Gen. 1:27) and God is love (1 John 4:8).

One of the most important goals in our life should be to know the love of God. Our second goal should be to live our lives in such a way that others will come to know God. Therefore, it is imperative that we learn to handle anger properly. Remember, anger is an emotion given to us by God to help us in our interactions with others. We can use anger to benefit the kingdom of God, or our sin nature can use it in a destructive manner.

James 1:2-3 says, "Consider it all joy, my brethren, when you encounter various trials; knowing that the testing of your faith produces endurance" (NASB). Trials and difficult circumstances, without sufficient faith, can provoke us to anger. Paul said, "Get rid of all bitterness, rage and anger, brawling and slander, along with every form of malice" (Eph. 4:31 NIV). He also spoke about the ungodly attitudes that are present when angry. Look at the sinful attitudes that go with ungodly anger: bitterness, wrath, clamor, slander, and malice. When we do not show and live God's love and His ways, our sin nature takes over and other wrong responses become evident in our lives. Matthew 5:22 says, "But I say to you that everyone who is angry with his brother shall be guilty before the court" (NASB). The worst expression of anger is murder. In 1 John 3:15, God equated hatred with murder.

Psalms 37:7-8 warns us that anger mishandled leads to evil-doing. James knew quick anger could lead us into serious problems, which is why he said, "Everyone should be quick to hear, slow to speak and slow to become angry" (James 1:19 NIV).

A person who becomes angry quickly is always a poor listener. "An angry man stirs up strife, and a hot-tempered man abounds in transgressions" (Prov. 29:22 NASB). Simply put, people given to chronic anger are likely to be troublemakers, thoughtless toward others, always caught up in spur-of-the-moment wrongdoing, and are often impulsive and compulsive.

> "Be angry, and yet do not sin; do not let the sun go down on your anger."
> (Eph. 4:26 NASB)

In his book *Good n' Angry*, Les Carter compares assertive anger with aggressive anger. He states "assertive anger is to put forward one's beliefs and values in a confident, self-assured manner."[11] This is the only form of anger Jesus used. An example of assertive anger occurred when Jesus encountered the moneychangers in the temple (Mark 11:15-17). He exposed their sin (selling in the temple and cheating the people). Jesus' anger was strong and forceful. Assertive anger always has a constructive conclusion. Jesus showed appropriate responses in the following ways:

- He expressed His anger without harboring feelings of hatred and bitterness.
- He was able to effectively continue teaching and ministering to the people immediately after expressing His anger.
- He communicated in a way that captured the people's attention.
- He did not go away plotting evil or feeling sorry for Himself.
- He carried on His tasks in a responsible manner.

The Bible tells us of Jesus being in the synagogue with religious leaders and a man with a withered hand. The Word says, "And when He had looked around at them with anger, being grieved by the hardness of their hearts, He said to the man, 'Stretch out your hand.'" (Mark 3:5 NKJV). The emotion that accompanied Jesus' anger was grief. His anger was a result of seeing people hurting. His love for people caused Him to be angry about what was happening to them as a result of man-made rules. He wanted them to see the rich fulfillment His love for them can bring rather than the emptiness produced by living by empty rules.

Carter states that aggressive anger "seeks to put forward one's beliefs about what one believes to be right. It is a direct reflection of the sin nature that exists within every person." He says, "This type of anger is abrasive, insensitive, inconsiderate, lacks empathy, and often leads to violence toward another person or object."[12] An example of aggressive anger can be seen when Jesus and His disciples were traveling to Jerusalem by way of Samaria. Jesus and His disciples were not allowed to stay in one of the towns. This angered the disciples and they said, "Lord, do you want us to call fire down from heaven to destroy them?" (Luke 9:54 NIV). Jesus did not become angry at the Samaritans for turning Him down, but did become angry with his disciples and rebuked them (Luke 9:55).

The disciples' anger was aggressive because it contained the following characteristics:

- They were motivated by spite, vengeance, bitterness, and hatred.

- Their anger had no useful function.
- They expressed a sense of superiority.
- They were not motivated by love.
- Their anger was destructive.
- They were only interested in their own needs.
- They wanted their needs met and did not consider others.

Remember, Jesus is our perfect example. We are to follow Him by being loving. Anger cannot control us or lead us into destructive behavior if we apply God's principles to our lives. We are to deal with our sin, get our hearts healed, and walk in His principles of love:

- Love is realistic, compassionate and understanding
- Love is unconditional (Rom. 5:8)
- Love is understanding/empathetic
- Love is forgiving (Matt. 18:22)
- Love recognizes that we are all equal (Rom. 3:23)
- Love is best stated in 1 Corinthians 13:4-7 (TLB):

> "Love is very patient and kind, never jealous or envious, never boastful or proud, never haughty or selfish or rude. It does not hold grudges and will hardly even notice when others do it wrong. It is never glad about injustice, but rejoices whenever truth wins out. If you love someone you will be loyal to him no matter what the cost. You will always believe in him, always expect the best of him, and always stand your ground in defending him."

God has given us the ability to choose how we will respond to situations and circumstances in our lives. We have a choice to respond in love or with aggressive anger. Angry people often respond to others using the behaviors listed below:

Verbal outbursts	Physical Attack	Stubbornness
Blame	Silent Treatment	Sarcasm
Criticism	Forgetfulness	Procrastination
Laziness	Gossip	Complaining
Half-hearted efforts	Preoccupation	Intimidation

Depression Use of drugs/alcohol Sexual sins

We have a choice of handling our anger in one of the three following ways:

1. Repression - ignore anger and it will go away. This form of denial pushes feelings into subconscious.
2. Expression - know when and how to express anger.
3. Release - conscious decision to let go of anger.

Repression and Christianity do not mix. God requires us to deal with our sin. Repression occurs when we ignore our sin and push our sinful attitudes and feelings into the subconscious. We deny they exist, but our behavior confirms their existence. Our anger is then exhibited in various inappropriate behaviors addressed above. We must choose to look at our anger and the repercussions it has produced in our lives.

Healing Invokes Several Steps

1. Identifying bitter-root judgments, bitter-root expectancies, and inner vows made as a child.
2. Identifying the lies we have learned to believe about ourselves.
3. Identifying false guilt and true guilt.
4. Obtaining a clear understanding of God's love for us.
5. Learning to apply the love principles in 1 Corinthians 13.
6. Learning about God's forgiveness toward us and our need to forgive others.
7. Applying forgiveness. (1 John 1:9, Matt. 6:14-15)
8. Attending an anger management support group to develop accountability for our behavior and commit to working through our anger issues.

The Word of God says, "Be ye therefore perfect, even as your Father which is in heaven is perfect" (Matt. 5:48 KJV). The word *perfect* is better translated as *mature.* In other words, we are to put ourselves into a maturing process, trying to live the love that is from God.

The Abuse Cycle Assignment

Below is a checklist to help you determine your level of anger. Check those characteristics that are true of you.

- ☐ My greatest struggles are with myself.
- ☐ Sometimes I try to convince myself that I am superior to others.
- ☐ When I make a mistake I tend to hate myself.
- ☐ I frequently battle feelings of guilt or condemnation.
- ☐ No matter how hard I try, I feel like a failure.
- ☐ At times I feel like life has taken more from me than it has given.
- ☐ There are times when I would like to run away.
- ☐ I seem to have abnormal sleep patterns.
- ☐ I struggle with my weight - gaining or losing too much.
- ☐ Life seems like the pits.
- ☐ When I talk about my irritations, I don't want to hear an opposite point of view.
- ☐ Criticism bothers me a great deal.
- ☐ I do not easily forget when someone does me wrong.
- ☐ I have many critical thoughts.
- ☐ Unimportant issues cause me undue stress and anxiety.
- ☐ I feel inwardly annoyed when family, friends and associates do not comprehend my needs.
- ☐ At times I seem to have an unusual amount of guilt even though it seems unnecessary.
- ☐ It seems I do more for others than they do for me.
- ☐ I have had many stormy or unstable relationships.
- ☐ I often feel restless on the inside.
- ☐ Sometimes I am so discouraged, I want to quit.
- ☐ I use sarcasm in expressing humor.
- ☐ I desire acceptance by others, but fear rejection.
- ☐ I am overly sensitive to rejection.
- ☐ I abandon others when they need me.
- ☐ I often take an "I don't care" attitude toward others in need.
- ☐ My conscience bothers me about things I have done in the past.

- ☐ I have had too many quarrels or disagreements with members of my family.
- ☐ I act kindly on the outside but am angry on the inside.
- ☐ Sometimes I say things to hurt others and really don't care.
- ☐ I like to tell people exactly what I think.
- ☐ I have a tendency to blame others for my problems.
- ☐ Many mornings I wake up feeling tired.
- ☐ When people are being unreasonable I usually take a strong dislike to them.
- ☐ Sometimes I am moody.
- ☐ People who know me well would say I am stubborn or strong-willed.
- ☐ When someone speaks ill of me, my natural response is to defend myself.
- ☐ People always seem to fail me.
- ☐ It is better to be alone than with others.
- ☐ I frequently feel like I will be rejected.
- ☐ I have problems controlling my sexual urges.
- ☐ I concern myself with others' opinions of me more than I like to admit.
- ☐ I don't like to admit to myself how angry I am.
- ☐ I have frequent physical problems.
- ☐ I often sulk and pout.
- ☐ As I speak my convictions, my voice becomes increasingly louder.
- ☐ If I don't like what someone does, I will be silent and not respond.
- ☐ Sometimes I use sarcasm in a very biting way.

If you have answered "yes" to 15 or more of the questions, you have a serious problem with anger.

1. Go back to the chapter on *Trust* and begin working through the hurt and pain from your childhood.
2. Work through the hurt and forgive all those who have offended you. Seek God's forgiveness for those you have hurt.
3. If you have worked through each chapter and still feel like anger has control of you, consider that you may need to deal with a spiritual demonic stronghold. If that is the case, find someone who understands this type of warfare and have him or her pray for you.

What ways do you most generally express your anger? (Example: rage, yelling, silent treatment, leaving the house)

Do you often feel belittled, rejected, or discounted? If so, by whom? Why do you think you feel this way? Explain.

What needs do you have?

How do you usually respond when your needs aren't met?

Are these needs others can meet or are you expecting others to give you only what God can give you? Give examples.

How do your unmet needs feed your anger?

What are the imperfections you have a hard time accepting?

Whom do you most often blame for your imperfections?

In what ways do you tend to express your imperfections or limitations?

How do you see yourself?

List the circumstances in your life that have made you angry.

Identify the people involved in those circumstances. Have you forgiven them? Can you respond to them in a loving and caring way? If not, you need to choose to forgive them.

How do you attempt to control others? Describe how you get others to do what you want them to do? How do you use fear and intimidation?

What areas of responsibility around the home do you fail to do when you are angry or upset with your spouse or children?

Do others complain about your attitude or behavior? If so, what do they complain about? How do you respond to them? Is it a Christ-like response?

Is your anger out of control? Ask those close to you and listen to their response.

Have you ever physically hit someone when you are angry? How often has this happened?

Do you sometimes call people names or insult them when you are angry? If so, how often do you do this and under what kind of circumstances?

Do you discuss your anger with others or do you only react privately?

Read over the scriptures describing a fool. What kind of person would you describe yourself to be?

Write a one to two page essay describing what type of person you become when you are angry.

When you have finished this assignment, look honestly at the depth of your anger. If it is a serious problem, find someone to pray with you over the hurts within your life. If you still struggle, you may need to seek professional help. The cycle of abuse and roots of anger need to be dealt with. According to the Bible the sins of the fathers are passed onto the third and fourth generation (Exod. 20:4-6).

Abusive Cycle Picture

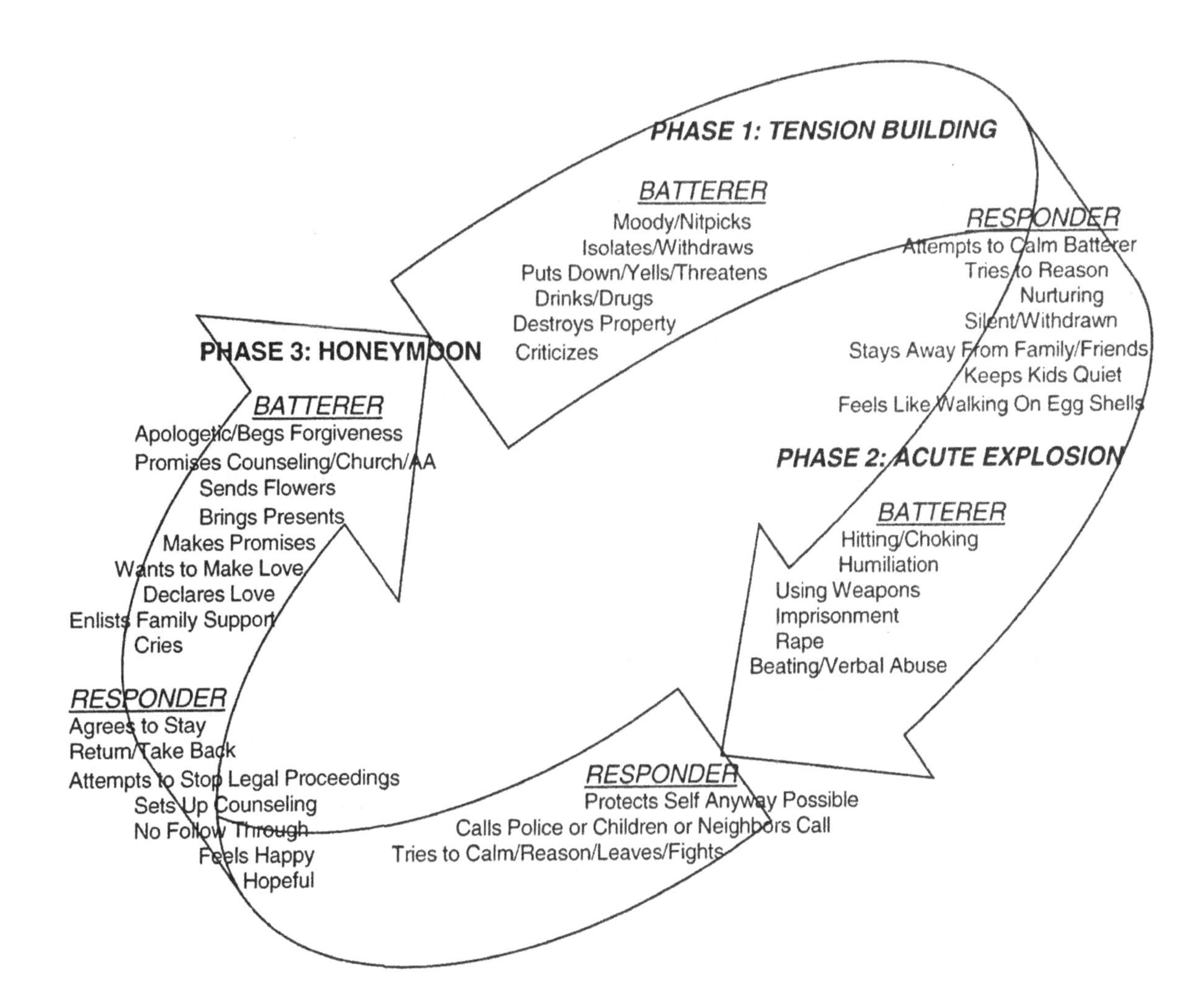

Depression

Depression can develop because of unresolved pain and unresolved feelings of anger. Depression may also be the result of a physical problem. There are different kinds of depression, and the treatment for each kind can vary extensively. Psychiatrists believe one form of depression is a reaction to something that has happened such as a serious illness, a death of a loved one or a friend, a traumatic experience, or physical or emotional pain.

One can suffer from a depressive disorder—even if there is no logical explanation for it. It seems as though nothing has happened that would make the person depressed. This form of depression is due to biochemical changes within the body, although nobody knows for sure what triggers the imbalance behind the depression.

Depression is a form of what is commonly known as a mood or affective disorder because it is primarily concerned with a change in one's mood.

Characteristics of Depression

- Loss of interest in, or the inability to take pleasure from activities that are normally enjoyed or found enjoyable by others, such as hiking, shopping, skiing, etc. The individual abandons or refuses to participate in activities they previously enjoyed. Loss of interest in sex may also be a sign of depression.
- Reduced ability to concentrate, which also causes impaired memory for everyday things, such as forgetting what you went to the kitchen for. This is not so much due to a defect in memory, but because a depressive's brain prevents him/her from remembering. Depressive brains are slow to process, so they need a lot of time to mentally process what is being said and how they are going to respond to another person or a situation. It is as though their brain is in slow motion.

Simple tasks like making the bed or cleaning the bathroom can require major effort and may even be abandoned because the task seems too difficult.

- Disturbed sleep. Many depressed people lack energy and become easily tired, yet do not sleep well at night. Others sleep for long periods of time.
- Appetites vary. Most depressives lose interest in food as well as everything else in their lives. Others find themselves craving carbohydrate foods. Weight varies depending on what they are eating.
- Reduced self-esteem and self-confidence. Many professionals believe that low self-esteem makes individuals susceptible to depression.
- Ideas of guilt and unworthiness. In severe depression, feelings of unworthiness and guilt may be accentuated by negative thoughts that say, "You are worthless and useless."
- Bleak, pessimistic, and hopeless view of the future. A depressed person tends to become extremely negative and has difficulty believing or seeing anything positive about the future. This is one of the major difficulties to overcome in the treatment of depression.
- Ideas or acts of self-harm or suicide. Because such individuals feel unworthy and the future seems bleak and hopeless, they may think of ways to commit suicide even if they do not plan on doing it. Some individuals may not consider suicide, but may physically harm themselves. An example would be cutting themselves with a knife or sharp object.
- Loss of feelings. They have lost the desire to express affection for or interest in others. They are emotionally flat and display minimal facial expression. They say words and thoughts without any feelings connected to them.
- Reduced tolerance. Some individuals find that they are less able to put up with noise and bright lights, causing them to become agitated or irritated. This may play a part in their further isolating themselves from others. As the depression becomes worse, isolation worsens.

All of these symptoms vary depending on the severity of the depression.

Mild Depression

Sufferers experience all or most of the above symptoms, but they are mild. Individuals are still able to carry on with their normal life. They may appear low in spirits and possibly less sharp in their thinking or in their interests. They continue to do essential tasks, but become upset when they do not feel they are coping well.

Moderate Depression

More depressive symptoms are present than are found in the mild. The depressed person's moods and behaviors are becoming more obvious to others. When a person is moderately depressed, he/she may find it difficult to work, both on the job and at home. Eventually the struggle may become so intense that the depressive abandons all efforts to do anything.

Severe Depression

When depression becomes severe, the individual cannot function with any degree of reliability. Severe depressives tend to lack any desire to talk to others or to look after themselves. They exhibit restlessness, hopelessness, and agitation over their situation, but can do nothing about it. Feelings of unworthiness and self-disgust will lead to severe negative self-talk. The negative self-talk may include thoughts that tell them they are no good and life isn't worth living. They become indifferent to the needs of their loved ones.

When people are suffering from major depression, they are less able to motivate themselves to do anything. On the other hand, those with mild or moderate depression feel that they are making a fuss about nothing, and they just have to "pull themselves together." They will make statements like, "What is wrong with me that I can't seem to function?" and "I don't care what happens to me or others." They hate how they are feeling, but can't seem to change their thoughts or behaviors.

In her book *Depression: Your Questions Answered,* Sue Breton says, "Depression has a very vicious downward spiral that sucks one in if one is not careful. The more depressed one feels, the less inclined one is to do anything positive and they sink deeper into the depression."[13] Getting the right kind of professional help is very important.

The following symptoms are found in those suffering from depression:

- Painful inability to experience pleasure
- Sadness
- Hopelessness
- Helplessness
- Decrease in energy level, sustained fatigue, many naps
- Lethargic
- Small tasks may seem difficult or impossible to accomplish

- Sense of worthlessness
- Guilt becomes excessive or inappropriate
- Slow thinking, difficulty in concentrating
- Indecisiveness
- Memory difficulty and easily distracted
- Not caring anymore

Various disorders that feature depression are as follows:

- Recurrent Brief Depression
- Masked Depression
- Seasonal Affective Disorder
- Anxiety
- Past Traumatic Stress Disorder
- Postnatal Depression
- Bereavement
- Brain Pathology
- Depressive Personality
- ADHD or ADD

What Causes Depression?

Heredity

Some forms of depression may be inherited. Bipolar or Manic Depression is a severe condition characterized by intense and often alternating moods. Unipolar depression is when one has lowered moods in varying degrees. Breton states in her book on depression that "one study has estimated that of people with no family history of bipolar or unipolar depression, only 1 in 100 will develop bipolar and 3 in 100 will develop the unipolar kind. On the other hand, among those people who do have a family history of unipolar depression, 1 in 10 will develop the disorder. If bipolar is in the family, 1 in 5 will develop it."[14]

Life Problems

- Aging and the difficulties of getting old, including health problems
- Women in menopause
- Individuals with serious illnesses

- Family crisis
- Drinking

Environment

- Individuals who lack a close relationship with parents
- Individuals who feel abandoned by their parents, especially their mother
- Individuals who have no close relationships from childhood to adulthood
- A bad marriage or conflicts in marriage
- Poor living conditions
- Financial problems
- Abusive relationships

The environment and the way an individual thinks about his/her situation plays the biggest factor in the development of depression.

Triggers

Most depressive disorders are brought on by unresolved hurtful issues from the past or extreme stress. However, some depressive disorders begin for seemingly no obvious reason.

Triggers may include:

- Biological or chemical change in the body which does not appear to be within the control of the individual
- Certain foods or allergies
- Imbalances caused by hormonal changes
- Changes in the individual's biochemistry brought about by the way he or she thinks and feels
- Poor nutrition

How a person thinks plays a major role in developing depression. A negative thinking pattern or unresolved painful life circumstances can lead to or keep a person in depression. If those hurtful conflicts are not resolved, the depression may worsen. A person's personality, their environment, and their coping mechanisms play a part in how quickly they can make choices that get them back on the road to wholeness. The way a person thinks, their facial expressions and body language may cause a chemical change in the center of the brain where emotions are controlled. Woundedness resulting in low self-esteem may cause one to feel they don't deserve anything good and that life will not go well for them. This belief system will not elevate the depression, but may cause the depression to get worse.

The Brain

In order to function, our entire system relies on messages being transmitted from the brain to the various parts of the body and back again. Dr. Breton explains the working of the brain as follows:

> "Neurotransmitters are the chemicals that help to send the messages to and from the brain. Electrical impulses carrying the messages are passed through the body along the nerves, from one nerve cell to another. The nerve cells are called neurons. Between one neuron and the next, however, there is a gap called a synapse. The impulse has to jump this gap to carry on. When it reaches the gap, neurotransmitters are released, allowing the message to cross.
>
> "The neurochemicals make it possible for the impulse containing the message to cross the gap. There must also be another neurochemical, called the receptor, on the other side of the gap to receive the message.
>
> "After a neurochemical has done its work, it has to be reabsorbed by the body. This is why exercise is beneficial to anxious people. Anxiety messages stimulate a particular chemical so that they can cross the gaps. Exercise rids the body of these neurotransmitter chemicals when they have done their job. Exercise thus helps control anxiety and has been found helpful for depression.
>
> "If the wrong neurotransmitters are being produced to bridge these gaps, or incompatible receptors are meeting them, then the body works inefficiently in some way and illness results. It is this that is the theory behind the belief that many psychiatric illnesses, especially depression, may one day be shown to be due to just such a defect."[15]
>
> "Many of the anti-depressants that are used are made up of substances designed to correct the imbalances that are thought to exist. The fact

> that they sometimes work and sometimes do not implies that one has to find the right drug for the imbalance in that person. Moreover, in the case of a disorder so closely tied in with one's thoughts and feelings, it is possible that other factors in the individual's life are causing the imbalance to continue in spite of all attempts to balance it out with drugs."[16]

Most individuals who suffer from depression also have sleep problems. Their circadian rhythm is out of balance causing them to not get adequate sleep. Some researchers believe that the key to depression lies in the disruption of the circadian rhythms. Their reasoning is that defects in the neurotransmitters cannot explain all the symptoms of depression, but a defect in the circadian system can. The jury is still out on whether the neurotransmitters or the circadian system contributes to depression. Maybe both play a critical part in depression. What is beneficial is that anti-depressant medication work on both the neurotransmitters and the circadian rhythms to lift depression.

How Does It Feel To Be Depressed?

Being depressed feels like falling into a huge black hole. Depressed people often feel as though they are trying to climb out of the hole, but they keep getting washed back down. The worst part is that every time they feel like they are getting out of the hole and hope surfaces, then they wind up being washed back down the hole again. After this happens time and time again, hopelessness consumes and life seems very bleak. They feel as if they have lost control of their life. Nothing makes sense anymore. Their world has been turned upside down, and they can't turn it right side up. Everything about life seems difficult, and they do not feel the same about things as they did before they were depressed.

People's ability to bounce back differs. Depressed people keep trying to bounce back, but eventually they just cannot do it anymore. Finally they arrive at not wanting to feel or try anymore. It is at this point that they may decide to get counseling. When depression is caused by a chemical imbalance, it is impossible for an individual to work on problems until the depression is alleviated. The depression may very likely require taking an anti-depressant. Therapy is difficult for the client because he/she keeps drifting into hopelessness and no longer cares what happens to them.

The feelings of hopelessness and helplessness usually happen when we feel life has disappointed or failed us, or when we feel we can't control our surroundings. Negative thoughts about our life will lead to body changes. The result is more negative thoughts, which in turn result in bodily changes. This is a vicious cycle that has to be broken before depression will lift.

People with depression who struggle with helplessness tend to expect someone to come up with an answer for them. Some individuals have a tendency to seek out answers for themselves which usually result in not getting adequate help. Others seek out those who will listen to their feelings of helplessness, hopelessness, and despair. They may want help, but they are unwilling to make the changes they need to get better. Others simply don't recognize that their problem is depression and will get whatever help is recommended for them to feel normal again.

Hopelessness locks a depressive in his own emotionless prison. When a person is hopeless they believe there is no answer to their situation. A person will always feel helpless before feeling hopeless. Breton says, "The inability to cope with life, whether because of stress, depression or cancer, is still a defect of the whole person. The causes and cures are related not only to either the mind or the body, but also to a very complicated interaction between the two. Nobody develops any of these problems through choice, although one may get all or any of them as a result of the way one thinks and behaves in response to what life throws at them. The problem is that society does not recognize this."[17]

Another area not often addressed is that a chemical imbalance in the brain can cause an individual to be very angry or verbally abusive. I have known individuals that were so abusive to their spouse and children that the family wanted nothing to do with that person. Often a divorce was desired. Once that individual got on an anti-depressant, the verbal abuse stopped. That person not only had to take his/her medication, but had to learn better coping and conflict resolution skills. They had to learn how to have a healthy relationship minus the anger and acting out.

Help for Depression

Those who suffer from depression have similar thought patterns. If they need and get medical help for their depression, then they can work on their problems. The following are common belief systems among those who suffer from depression:

- There is something wrong with me.
- I am defective.
- I don't deserve to be happy.
- I am worthless.

- I am a failure
- Nothing I ever do is right or good enough.
- Life is not fair.
- I guess I deserve this as I don't really matter.

Depressed people are unable to believe that anyone would want to put themselves out on their account or do anything nice for them unless they have an ulterior motive. Depressed people are totally unable to believe that they have any worth. They expect nothing of themselves and often nothing from others. Overcoming depression lies in developing self-esteem and knowing who you are in God.

The way out of depression oftentimes lies in becoming angry enough over what has happened in our life. Next, we need to personally take responsibility for everything we have done, how we feel, and how we control our own thought life. It is our own thoughts that control how we look at life and handle situations. It is not what happens to us that controls us.

Depressed people's aim should be to develop awareness of what they really like, how they really feel, and what they really value. In order to do this, they have to allow themselves freedom to evaluate their thoughts and feelings. Deep feelings of shame often hinder them from doing this.

A good rule is allowing ourselves to see something positive in everything that happens to us. We should make the choice to use positive self-talk when a situation or negative feelings arises. Philippians 4:8 says to think on things that are true, noble, right, pure, lovely and admirable. Find scripture from God's Word that speaks of our value, worth and promise of an abundant life.

To come into healing, one has also to be willing to look at past woundedness and allow Jesus to heal those wounds and set us free. Looking at our hurts can be very scary, but Jesus will always walk with us through our healing and bring us into victory. Trust Him to do it. Remember God sees our depression and He died so that we could be healed! Claim it!

TIME IS NEVER THE ENEMY OF GOD'S PROMISES.

Depression Assignment

Do you struggle with feelings of sadness, helplessness or hopelessness?

How long have you felt this way?

Are their members in your family that have problems with depression or is there a history of depression among past family members? If so, who?

Are you angry? If so, do you express or suppress your anger?

Do others see you as depressed? Ask them to describe your mood swings to you.

If you have journaled and worked through hurt or anger issues from your past, consider seeing a medical doctor for treatment.

This book has been written to help individuals come into wholeness—taking us on a journey that starts in childhood and goes through adulthood. Our present day struggles have their roots in unresolved offenses and pain from the past. As we work through offenses and pains, we can come into healing. In each section, I addressed issues that are common in society today. God's people are wounded warriors who are often not as effective as they should be for the Kingdom of God. Let us walk into wholeness so that we can battle the enemy of our soul effectively and see ourselves and others set free. God bless you on your journey!

FEELING LIST

Loved
Valued
Encouraged
Exuberant
Cheerful
Relieved
Appreciated
Admired
Accepted
Fulfilled
Elated
Disheartened
Disappointed
Inadequate
Discouraged
Ashamed
Lonely
Neglected
Abandoned
Degraded
Betrayed
Despised
Isolated
Alienated
Slighted
Lost
Disenchanted
Tranquil
Ridiculed
Resentful
Smothered
Disgusted
Deceived
Regretful
Deprived
Cheated
Displeased
Unsure
Anxious
Doubtful
Grievous
Demoralized
Unloved
Pitiful
Humiliated
Tormented
Bewildered
Worthless
Vengeful
Afraid
Enraged
Hostile
Exhausted
Hopeless
Condemned
Depressed
Threatened
Tense
Misunderstood
Controlled
Irritated
Resigned
Coerced
Dismayed
Apathetic
Reluctant
Perplexed
Empty
Burdened
Condemned
Unwanted
Discarded
Vulnerable
Trapped
Desperate
Crushed
Hateful
Fearful
Seething
Defeated
Helpless
Outraged
Rejected
Hopeless

Resources

Sue Breton, *Depression: Your Questions Answered* (Element Books, 1996).

John and Paula Sandford, *The Transformation of the Inner Man* (Tulsa: Victory House, 1982).

Les Carter and Frank Minirth, *The Anger Workbook* (Nashville: Thomas Nelson, 1993).

Theo Johnson and Evelyn Diment, *Freedom Now* (Dealing Touch Ministries, 1994).

Workbook Order Form

To get copies of this workbook, order from:

Sydney Gienty
6428 Miner Dr. S. W.
Tumwater, Washington 98512

Cost. $24.95 plus shipping and handling.

To schedule or obtain additional information on seminars and/or workshops call 1-360-561-8577.

Endnotes

[1] This quote was taken from a seminar given by John and Paula Sandford in 1985 in Seattle, Washington.

[2] Ibid.

[3] John and Paula Sandford, *The Transformation of the Inner Man* (Tulsa: Victory House, 1982), 237.

[4] Ibid, 258.

[5] This quote was taken from a seminar given by John and Paula Sandford in 1985 in Seattle, Washington.

[6] Ibid.

[7] Ibid.

[8] Floyd McClung. Jr., *The Father Heart of God* (Eugene: Harvest, 2004).

[9] Patrick J. Carnes, *Out of the Shadows* (Center City: Hazelden, 2009).

[10] Quote taken from *Marriage Today* broadcast by Jimmy Evans in 2016.

[11] Les Carter, *Good 'n Angry* (Bloomington: Baker, 1983).

[12] Ibid.

[13] Sue Breton, *Depression: Your Questions Answered* (Element Books, 1996).

[14] Ibid.

[15] Ibid.

[16] Ibid.

[17] Ibid.

Printed in the United States
By Bookmasters